The Complete ASSET PROTECTION Guide

Arnold S. Goldstein

Enterprise Publishing, Inc.   Wilmington, DE

Contents

How to Use This Book

1

If you are like most people you are rightfully concerned about the exposure of your hard-earned personal and family assets to potential creditor claims. The threat of being sued for any one of countless reasons must be expected in today's litigious society. The risks are greatly increased if you are a professional or self-employed. But the dangers to your personal assets can strike from many directions. Lawsuits are only one danger. You may suddenly face a divorce, be hit by a huge tax deficiency or simply run up many more debts than you can afford, due to an unexpected job layoff or other financial emergency beyond your control.

These harsh realities lead many people to ask how they can lawfully minimize the possibility of losing their home, retirement pension, savings or other valuable assets to creditor claims.

This book was prepared to provide answers to these timely and critical questions. In doing so, this book will show you how to protect your assets legally and effectively. In other words, you will learn how to become "judgement proof" so that you are shielded by your own financial fortress.

This book also has two other com-

pelling purposes. First, it will highlight many causes of liability — those problem areas often overlooked by business people and professionals alike. In short, you will learn how to *avoid liability* and how to reduce the risk of a financial catastrophe.

Second, this book will demonstrate the many proven ways to remove threats to your property by reducing, settling and discharging any existing or potential liability on terms that are advantageous to you.

The Complete Asset Protection Guide has been designed for just about anyone with any property or assets worth protecting. Whether you are a businessperson or professional with a substantial net worth, or a young wage earner just starting out, this guide will show you the proven ways to safeguard your property from the inevitable financial hazards of life. This guide will be equally useful to attorneys, financial planners and other professionals who are increasingly asked to develop an intelligent and effective asset protection strategy for their clients.

In order to insure that you are not foreclosed from using any meaningful protective tool, this book will describe the benefits (and drawbacks) of the various protection techniques. As you review these techniques, it will become clear that some are particularly attractive for your situation and that others are not. Keep in mind that there is no one approach that will work for everyone — each person's situation is somewhat unique. What you must do is pick and choose those techniques that fit your needs. But, before you implement any of these techniques, we strongly urge you to consult your personal legal counsel. As you will see, laws vary from state to state; before you set a process in motion, you will want to be certain that your state laws allow the result you want.

A financial protection plan can take many different forms and has more than one purpose. So, for example, your immediate concern may be to protect your assets from creditors and lawsuits. But, when you design your fortress against liability, you will also be making decisions that will have tax and estate planning implications. Because these factors should be contemplated when you design your overall plan, this book will provide many tax and estate planning tips as it reviews each protective technique. Keep in mind, however, that the overriding purpose of this book is to show you how to protect your assets during your lifetime so that you may continue to enjoy the fruits of your la-

bor. For that reason, the primary emphasis of this book is on asset protection and not estate or tax planning. But, it should also be clear that when you safeguard your assets during your lifetime, you also maximize the estate you will leave to your heirs.

A financial protection plan can take many different forms. Lawsuit or creditor protection is usually only one objective. Tax considerations and estate planning will also influence your decisions. Although these factors must be considered, this book covers neither tax nor estate planning in depth as they are separate subjects too complex for full treatment here. Nevertheless, you will find many tax and estate planning tips and suggestions to incorporate into your asset protection strategy.

We recommend that you first review the book to obtain a better understanding of the asset protection strategies available to you. The sample legal forms at the end of each chapter are generally representative of those used in practice, but they are intended to simply familiarize you with the numerous asset protection tools. They are not suggested for self-use. Armed with this guide, however, you will work far more confidently and effectively with your counsel in designing the specific asset protection program that's just right for you and your family.

Asset Protection Planning

2

Why You Must Protect Yourself Today

It is indeed an unpleasant thought that a sudden lawsuit or financial reversal can cause you to lose your home, life savings and other valuable assets. Yet the realities are that it happens each and every day. Thousands of families and individuals fail to protect their assets, or plan for possible financial difficulties and find themselves wiped out, often with little warning.

How can you prepare yourself for financial disaster? First, be aware of the many possible sources of liability that most people encounter no matter how cautiously or prudently they may act:

- A motor vehicle accident.

- An accident in or around your home or business.

- An accident or injury caused by someone else for whom you are responsible such as an employee, partner, subcontractor or even a child or family member.

- Something happening on the job.

- Inability to fulfill an important contract.

- Default on a lease, purchase agreement or loan.

- Professional malpractice.

- Negligence as an officer or director of a corporation.

- Business debts for which you are personally responsible.

- Tax claims.

- Fines or governmental levies such as environmental protection violation assessments.

- Divorce or separation.

The list, of course, can go on endlessly, but the point is that no matter how safe and secure your financial situation may appear today, you can never be absolutely certain that your hard earned assets won't be in jeopardy tomorrow.

What is most unfortunate is that most families *lose* substantial assets when creditor claims arise. Yet any family can legally and effectively *save* its assets if only it takes timely and decisive action to fully protect its property no matter what type of legal or financial threat may arise.

Ten Rules for Asset Protection Planning

How can you protect your personal and family assets from financial disaster? Here are the 10 essential rules to follow:

Rule 1: Act Now

How your family's wealth is owned is something which you must plan *before* liability is incurred. Generally speaking, it will be too late if you wait until you have a substantial claim against you to do something. Advance planning is much more likely to withstand a challenge than would a last minute transfer of assets. If you now face a claim or potential liability of any concern, then seek immediate advice before the claim ripens into judgment and seizure of your assets. Remember this key point. Timely action *before* you have a problem is the most important ingredient for successful asset protection planning.

Rule 2: Update Your Planning

Make asset planning a continuous event. Review your program at least annually to insure you remain fully protected. Your financial affairs constantly change. You continually acquire new assets and dispose of existing assets. The risks to which you are exposed may change. Your financial objectives and priorities never remain the same. Then too, frequent changes in tax laws and even laws relating to asset protection strategies may necessitate a modified plan. Only a thorough and periodic review of your plan with your advisors can insure a plan that continues to best match your situation.

Rule 3: Expect Tradeoffs

Strategies used to insulate assets against creditor claims involve a number of tradeoffs. As a general rule, your creditors can attach whatever property you have to the extent of your rights in the property. If you own it, your creditors can seize your interest in it. Conversely, to effectively place control over an asset beyond the reach of creditors, you must also place it out of your control. You must be willing to surrender some control over assets you now completely control. This is an unfortunate but necessary part of asset protection. Most people agree, however, that the degree of control they may have lost was a small price to pay for the protection they gained.

Rule 4: Prioritize Objectives

Although this book focuses on deployment of assets for asset protection purposes, the strategies you will use also have tax and estate planning consequences. Frequently an asset protection technique offers significant tax and estate planning advantages as well, but that is not always the case. Your best asset protection strategy may present adverse tax consequences or interfere with the ideal disposition of your estate. Decide which of these factors is most important to you. Qualify the advantages and identify disadvantages of each. Once prioritized, candidly communicate your objectives to your advisors so they can design a plan to best meet those objectives.

Rule 5: Make Planning A Family Affair

Most heads of households view their property as belonging to the family rather than as an individual asset. The fact that the breadwinner earned the money that bought the family home and other assets does not mean that other family members have no right to these assets. Make asset protection planning a family affair. Once family members understand why assets are deployed as they are, there will be less resentment, uncertainty or questioning and far greater harmony within the family. Similarly, owners of a controlling interest in a business should involve minority interest partners in business planning for the same reasons. Communication and the sharing of objectives and concerns between those with an interest in the protection of assets is important for smooth implementation of the financial plan.

Rule 6: Commitment Needed

Asset protection plans often involve significant time and expense. For example, there may be considerable legal and accounting fees and various filing fees as well as additional paperwork involved in establishing or maintaining some of the entities described in this book. Understand these costs before embarking on any plan. Discuss costs and what will be required under a proposed plan *before* you agree to it. Be practical. Make certain the costs are proportionate to the value of the assets to be protected.

Rule 7: There's No One Right Plan

Within this book you will discover a variety of asset protection tools and strategies. Trusts, joint ownerships, partnerships, corporations and many other forms of ownership each offer certain advantages and disadvantages in the asset protection arsenal. This book will review each weapon in that arsenal. But, keep in mind that there is no one best strategy that fits everyone's needs. Everyone's situation is different. We all have different priorities, financial situations, family relationships. These differences create different purposes with respect to tax and estate planning, our overall financial objectives and our willingness to take on risks. On top of those differences, it should be noted that each state has its own debtor-creditor laws, and that those laws are not uniform.

As you read on, you will discover that this book anticipates each of those differences, and gives you a host of options from which you can pick and choose in order to design the plan that best fits your circumstances. That plan, however, should be implemented only after you review it with your attorney who can tell you whether the options you have chosen are effective under the laws of your state.

Rule 8: Find The Right Professional Team

By reading this book, you will soon appreciate why asset protection requires close guidance and a cooperative effort between your attorney, accountant or tax advisor, financial planner and even your insurance agent. Each brings to the planning process special professional skills.

Because asset protection has as its prime objective the insulation of assets from creditor claims, choosing the right attorney for professional assistance is essential for success. Select your legal advisor carefully. Not all attorneys are thoroughly familiar with debtor-creditor laws or asset protection strategies. Just as you would seek a criminal lawyer or divorce lawyer should you be involved with criminal or divorce problems, it is equally wise to engage a legal specialist experienced in financial protection and debtor-creditor law. Your family lawyer may be able to refer you to such a specialist, if not, consult your local bar association.

Rule 9: Be Prepared

Start now to inventory your various assets and assemble the numerous legal and financial documents your advisors will certainly want to review. These include:

- Your will, trusts or other estate documents

- Deeds and mortgages to real estate

- IRA, pension or retirement plans

- Trusts or wills in which you are a beneficiary

- Inventory of valuable personal property (jewelry, art, boats, etc.)

- Life insurance policies

- Stocks, bonds or other securities

- Notes or other obligations due you

- Savings accounts

- Ownership interests in family or closely held businesses

- Tax returns for prior three years

- Pending lawsuits or other claims against you

- Loans or other significant obligations to which you are indebted

- Prenuptial or postnuptial agreements

For your convenience, all of the forms you will need to inventory and list your various assets are found at the end of this chapter. Also, complete the net worth statement to accurately reflect your financial position.

Rule 10: *Asset Protection Is Both Lawful And Smart*

Deploying your assets to provide maximum protection from creditors is neither immoral nor unlawful. You have an obligation to yourself and your family to protect and preserve what you have worked so hard to accumulate. But we underscore the importance of a legal, defendable plan that can withstand challenge as opposed to a sham or fraudulent transfer, discussed in the next section, that can only leave you as vulnerable as before you started.

Avoid Fraudulent Transfers

Once a creditor seeks collection against you, you may then attempt to protect assets by secreting or by transferring them to third parties. Typically, such transfers are for less than a fair payment to the debtor, and almost always with a "string" attached to allow the debtor to reclaim the property after the financial difficulties have disappeared.

People concerned about protecting assets from creditors' claims are often told to "put everything in the name of someone else." Giving your assets to somebody else may appear the quickest and most sensible way of protecting yourself from a judgment. But that is seldom a prudent course of action. Simply transferring assets into the name of your spouse or friend does not always work. The law is not so naive as to allow a person to avoid payment of debts by making "gifts" of his assets to family members or friends. A person heavily in debt who suddenly gives his assets away for little or nothing seldom succeeds in placing those assets beyond the reach of creditors.

That does not mean, however, that a debtor cannot in many cases safely and legally transfer assets to his spouse, a trust for family members or for the benefit of third persons. The determination of whether a transfer of assets is "fraudulent" or lawful is a question of fact which courts decide in each case after considering a number of factors.

First, transfers are tested under the state statute that protects creditors. The basic law providing these rights is the Uniform Fraudulent Conveyance Act (UFCA) which has been adopted in: Arizona, California, Delaware, Idaho, Maryland, Massachusetts, Michigan, Minnesota, Montana, Nevada, New Hampshire, New Jersey, New Mexico, New York, North Dakota, Ohio, Oklahoma, Pennsylvania, South Dakota, Tennessee, Utah, Virgin Islands, Washington, Wisconsin, and Wyoming.

The most recent adoption occurred in 1969. In the above states, this is the basic state statutory law on fraudulent transfers. Hawaii, North Dakota and Oregon follow the Uniform Fraudulent Transfers Act (UFTA). Other states have comparable state statutes or rely on common law case decisions, which in all instances conform closely to the law established by the UFCA, and for discussion purposes grant creditors equivalent rights.

There is no federal statute dealing with fraudulent transfers. Therefore, the Internal Revenue Service and other federal agencies that may be creditors in an action must adopt the law of the state in which the debtor resides or the lawsuit commenced. In many instances this is the state where the property subject to claim is actually located.

The general rule is that before a transaction may be attacked as fraudulent there must be actual prejudice to the rights of the complaining creditor.

Two types of fraudulent conveyance are recognized.

1. *Fraud-in-Law* — where the nature of the transaction or agreement relating to the conveyance creates a conclusive presumption in law that the conveyance is fraudulent.

2. *Fraud-in-Fact* — where there is actual fraudulent intent to hinder and delay creditors.

Fraud-in-Law:

Generally, fraud-in-law exists when the following elements are present: (1) a sale or gift for less than fair value, (2) there existed an actual or anticipated liability, and (3) retention of insufficient assets by the debtor to fully pay and satisfy the liability.

Notice that there is no need for the creditor to establish actual motive or intent to hinder the creditor. The creditor is not obligated to prove evil intent but only the existence of the three elements. An example, would be a husband who transfers most of his assets to a trust for the benefit of his wife when a liability existed (or could reasonably be anticipated) prior to the transfer. If the creditor is unable to satisfy his claim from the husband's remaining assets, the creditor could successfully attach the asset transfer as it meets the three tests, even though the husband may have had no actual intent to defraud the creditor.

Fraud-in-Fact:

When relying upon fraud-in-fact to set aside a fraudulent conveyance, courts will look for certain "badges of fraud" or elements. These "badges" must be examined in context to all the circumstances surrounding the transfer before a court can infer fraudulent intent.

The following elements may be investigated by creditors, and considered by the courts to infer a fraudulent conveyance.

1. The fact that property was transferred by the debtor during a pending suit or after the debtor could reasonably anticipate a claim.

2. The transfer of all or substantially all of the debtor's assets so as to render the debtor insolvent or unable to satisfy creditor's claims.

3. The unexplained or unusual retention of possession of the property transferred by the debtor.

4. Transactions which are not in the ordinary course of business or are conveyed on terms or conditions that are uncharacteristic of the debtor.

5. The existence of a close family or friendship relationship between the debtor and transferee.

6. The debtor retaining a beneficial interest in the property or a future right to reacquire the property.

7. Failure to record a conveyance or unusual lapse in time prior to recording.

8. Failure of the buyer to take reasonably prudent steps before acquiring the property.

9. Failure of either the debtor or the transferee to produce evidence or otherwise cooperate in any judicial examination of the conveyance.

10. An inadequate or fictitious consideration or the false recital of consideration which, in fact, was not paid.

You'll notice that several "badges of fraud" are the same elements as used in a "fraud-in-law" claim. In addition to these particular elements of fraud, many other factors, individually or collectively, may be viewed by courts as badges of fraud. Some of these factors include:

1. The parties failure to keep proper records concerning financial transactions between them.

2. Alteration or attempted alteration of the dates or other terms of conveyance.

3. The debtors transfer of money out of the country.

4. Failure to enforce rights under a contract or demand payment of monies due under the conveyance.

5. Resale of the assets by the buyer soon after purchase and for an amount considerably more than the purchase price.

The underlying characteristic of most fraudulent transfers is that the debtor never really intended to transfer ownership or control of the assets. The most obvious example is a sale where the buyer agrees to hold title in his own name but with the understanding the asset continues to belong to the debtor and will be reconveyed to the debtor upon request. This type transaction, or course, is nothing more than a sham and will likely be considered invalid against pursuing creditors.

Of course, there are situations where the fraudulent intent of the debtor is not present or may be impossible to prove. For example, a debtor may simply give property to a friend, relative, or person in need for purely benign or charitable purposes. The debtor may make a "gift" of property or conduct a "bargain sale" of possessions to either raise ready cash, or with the hope or understanding that the property may be repurchased at a later date. Then again, a debtor may sell or otherwise convey property for less than fair value while engaged in an undercapitalized business or transaction, but with no intent to reacquire the property. As you can see, whether a transfer is fraudulent and can be set aside by a creditor depends on many facts, and thus presents a complicated area of law and one not always subject to certain answers.

The classic example of a presumed-in-law fraudulent transfer is when an insolvent debtor simply gives away his property to his children, getting nothing in return. The theory is that property owned by an insolvent, although formally titled in the insolvent debtor's name, in equity really belongs to his creditors. Thus, if the debtor transfers away that property without getting a reasonably equivalent commercial exchange in return, then this is so prejudicial to creditors, who in equity own the property, that the law will give those creditors a remedy. The law will permit the creditors to get their property back, even though they cannot prove that the transferor had any evil intent to cheat them when he made the transfer. The result would remain the same even if it could be shown that the transferor had benign or charitable motives in transferring the property.

Tip

Equivalent commercial exchange of "fair value" doesn't necessarily mean the transferee pay the full market price for the asset. Generally, a payment of at least 70% of the fair value is considered adequate consideration to destroy a claim of fraudulent transfer.

Prior case decisions have given us some general guidelines as to what might constitute a fair consideration. However, there might be instances where the market value of the property is so well-known and so easily attainable that even a small deviation from the fair market value might be considered less than a reasonably equivalent exchange and thus a fraudulent transfer.

Consider, for example, publicly listed securities which can be sold on the public exchanges at a known and given price on any day of the week. If a debtor does not obtain close to the listed market price then it could be successfully argued that a reasonably equivalent exchange had not occurred.

Conversely, there might be assets difficult to market or which have limited appeal and are subject to distress sale. In such cases, should a debtor obtain 50% of the fair market value, the courts may well be justified in accepting that as fair consideration under the circumstances.

In short, what constitutes a fair consideration or a reasonably equivalent exchange depends upon the individual circumstances of the case. The 70% rule should be used as a good rule of thumb keeping in mind that there are acceptable variations on the up side as well as down side, acceptable depending upon the actual circumstances of the case.

To successfully attack a fraudulent conveyance a creditor or trustee in a state of bankruptcy must cross two obstacles. First, there must be proof of the debtor's fraudulent intent — either actual or constructive. But this is not enough. As a second step, it must be proven that the transferee also acted in bad faith when the property was obtained.

Under Section 9 of the Uniform Fraudulent Conveyance Act, a transferee is completely protected if he acts in good faith and pays equivalent value. In other words, not even if the transfer by the debtor is clearly fraudulent on his part, there is no action a creditor or trustee can take if the transferee who now holds the property is a "good faith buyer."

Who is this good faith transferee who is protected from fraudulent transfer attack? A transferee who qualifies as a bona fide purchaser can keep the property free of the trustee's or creditor's claim to it (even though the transferor fraudulently conveyed it to this transferee) if three conditions are met:

1.   The transferee acquires the property in good faith.

2.   The transferee takes the property without knowledge of the fraud on creditors that the transferor actually or constructively sought to perpetrate.

3.   The transferee gives fair consideration (as previously discussed).

What if a transferee satisfies only two of the three elements set forth above? Perhaps a transferee acts in good faith and he acts without knowledge of the fraud being perpetrated on the transferor's creditors. He does, however, bargain too hard and ends up paying less than fair consideration. In such a case the transferee must give up the property to the creditors or trustee, but retains a lien on the property to permit him to be reimbursed for the consideration he actually paid. In other words, a transferee who bargains too hard loses the benefit of his bargain. The court considers that bargain too unfair to the creditors to be tolerated even in our free market society.

The Rights of Creditors

Fraudulent conveyance law is, of course, designed to protect creditors from debtors who improperly transfer their assets to avoid creditors' claims. A creditor pursuing a delinquent debt or claim would first reduce the claim against the debtor to a judgment. While enforcing the judgment, the creditor may discover that the debtor has earlier disposed of assets in a way which now hinders, or precludes satisfaction of the creditor's judgment. The creditor would then have to rely upon the remedies available under various fraudulent conveyance statutes.

Once a judgment creditor proves that the transfer or conveyance made by the debtor is fraudulent, the creditor may attach or levy execution directly upon the property in the hands of the debtor's grantee, or the creditor may instead annul the debtor's con-

veyance and proceed directly against the debtor or the property as if the conveyance had never been made.

Fraudulent conveyance law also provides provisional or emergency remedies for creditors whose claim against the debtor is not yet reduced to judgment, or whose claim is not even mature, fixed or liquidated. Under fraudulent conveyance law such individuals qualify as "creditors." When such a creditor discovers the debtor has transferred property in a manner which will ultimately hinder the creditor's collection efforts once the claim is mature or reduced to a judgment, that creditor may seek preliminary relief. This relief may be in the form of an injunction or restraining order, receivership, attachment, or similar remedy that would freeze the asset for the benefit of the creditor.

Since a conveyance made by a debtor with intent to hinder, delay, or defraud creditors is fraudulent, as is every conveyance for less than fair consideration payment by a debtor who intends to incur debts beyond his ability to pay those debts as they mature, creditors are entitled to the relief of setting aside the conveyance or levying on the property as if the conveyance had never been made.

This does not mean that these rights will necessarily be exercised.

Just as it is costly for a debtor to defend against a claim of fraudulent conveyance, it is equally costly for a creditor to pursue such a claim. Many creditors are likely to go quietly away once they realize they are up against a judgement-proof debtor. Many may not investigate whether the debtor engaged in fraudulent conveyances. Others don't consider it cost-justified to pursue such a claim and may settle for far less than they would against a debtor with "deep pockets." Other creditors, such as the Internal Revenue Service, are often too bureaucratic in their collection efforts. Although they have the right and machinery to chase fraudulent conveyances, they do far less often then you might expect.

Key Tips to Remember

Tip 1. Whether a transfer was in contemplation of a creditor claim is a key element in a fraudulent transfer claim. Therefore, it is essential that you judgment proof your assets well in advance of legal or financial difficulties.

Tip 2. Avoid dealings with close relatives. Interfamily transactions are naturally suspect and vulnerable to attack. Transfers to non-family members or business associates are less likely to be challenged.

Tip 3. Document consideration adequately. If you owe money to a friend or relative, formalize the debt with binding promissory notes. If the debt is based on services, keep adequate records to support the fact services were rendered. Maintain a paper trail to support your transaction.

Tip 4. Always time your transfers to prove a legitimate reason for the transfer. You should have reasons apart from sheltering assets for making the transfer. Making transfers to family members as birthday gifts, for example, indicates reasons other than a mere sheltering of assets. Insure that your transfer has an "innocent" purpose and you will obtain maximum protection.

Tip 5. Seek advice from professional counselors. For example, advice from your attorney to transfer your assets to your spouse for estate planning purposes can help negate inference of fraudulent intent on your part.

Tip 6. Incremental or periodic small transfers are less likely to be challenged than would transfers of one or two significant assets. It is less likely that courts will overturn transfers of different types of assets to many different transferees than they are to the transfer to one transferee.

Tip 7. Never participate in any scheme or plan to conceal assets from creditors, or in a bankruptcy case. While fraudulent transfers are only civil proceedings, the intentional concealment of assets or false statements in regard to owned assets can have serious criminal consequences. Remember, there is a fine line distinction between lawful asset protection and unlawful asset concealment. Follow your attorney's advice to defend the action you take.

Tip 8. The UFCA does not have its own statute of limitation. States generally have a 3 to 6 year limitations period during which actions to invalidate fraudulent conveyances may be brought. Under Section 548 of the Bankruptcy Code, the bankruptcy trustee may only reach transfers made within one year of the filing of the bankruptcy petition. This is one of the major differences between the provisions of the UFCA and the Bankruptcy Code. However, a bankruptcy trustee can elect to proceed under state law and thus have the benefit of the longer statute of limitations. This underscores another important reason why you should protect assets well in advance of a financial problem.

UNIFORM FRAUDULENT CONVEYANCE ACT

Sec. 1. Definition of Terms. In this act "Assets" of a debtor means property not exempt from liability for his debts. To the extent that any property is liable for any debts of the debtor, such property shall be included in his assets.

"Conveyance" includes every payment of money, assignment, release, transfer, lease, mortgage or pledge of tangible or intangible property, and also the creation of any lien or encumbrance.

"Creditor" is a person having any claim, whether matured or unmatured, liquidated or unliquidated, absolute, fixed or contingent.

"Debt" includes any legal liability, whether matured or unmatured, liquidated or unliquidated, absolute, fixed or contingent.

Sec. 2. Insolvency.

(1) A person is insolvent when the present fair salable value of his assets is less than the amount that will be required to pay his probable liability on his existing debts as they become absolute and matured.

(2) In determining whether a partnership is insolvent there shall be added to the partnership property the present fair salable value of the separate assets of each general partner in excess of the amount probably sufficient to meet the claims of his separate creditors, and also the amount of any unpaid subscription to the partnership of each limited partner, provided the present fair salable value of the assets of such limited partner is probably sufficient to pay his debts, including such unpaid subscription.

Sec. 3. Fair Consideration. Fair consideration is given for property, or obligation,

(a) When in exchange for such property, or obligation, as a fair equivalent therefor, and in good faith, property is conveyed or a previous debt is satisfied, or

(b) When such property, or obligation is received in good faith to secure a present advance or antecedent debt in amount not disproportionately small as compared with the value of the property, or obligation obtained.

Sec. 4. Conveyances by Insolvent. Every conveyance made and every obligation incurred by a person who is or will be thereby rendered insolvent is fraudulent as to creditors without regard to his actual intent if the conveyance is made or the obligation is incurred without a fair consideration.

Sec. 5. Conveyances by Persons in Business. Every conveyance made without fair consideration when the person making it is engaged or is about to engage in a business or transaction for which the property remaining in his hands after the conveyance is an unreasonably small capital, is fraudulent as to creditors and as to other persons who become creditors during the continuance of such business or transaction without regard to his actual intent.

Sec. 6. Conveyances by a Person about to Incur Debts. Every conveyance made and every obligation incurred without fair consideration when the person making the conveyance or entering into the obligation intends or believes that he will incur debts beyond his ability to pay as they mature, is fraudulent as to both present and future creditors.

Sec. 7. Conveyance Made with Intent to Defraud. Every conveyance made and every obligation incurred with actual intent, as distinguished from intent presumed in law, to hinder, delay, or defraud either present or future creditors, is fraudulent as to both present and future creditors.

Sec. 8. Conveyance of Partnership Property. Every conveyance of partnership property and every partnership obligation incurred when the partnership is or will be thereby rendered insolvent, is fraudulent as to partnership creditors, if the conveyance is made or obligation is incurred

(a) To a partner, whether with or without a promise by him to pay partnership debts, or

(b) To a person (not a partner) without fair consideration to the partnership as distinguished from consideration to the individual partners.

Sec. 9. Rights of Creditors Whose Claims Have Matured.

(1) Where a conveyance or obligation is fraudulent as to a creditor, such creditor, when his claim has matured, may, as against any person except a purchaser for fair consideration without knowledge of the fraud at the time of the purchase, or one who has derived title immediately from such a purchaser,

(a) Have the conveyance set aside or obligation annulled to the extent necessary to satisfy his claim, or

(b) Disregard the conveyance and attach or levy execution upon the property conveyed.

(2) A purchaser who without actual fraudulent intent has given less than a fair consideration for the conveyance or obligation, may retain the property or obligation as security for repayment.

Sec. 10. Rights of Creditors Whose Claims Have Not Matured. Where a conveyance made or obligation incurred is fraudulent as to a creditor whose claim has not matured he may proceed in a court of competent jurisdiction against any person against whom he could have proceeded had his claim matured, and the court may,

(a) Restrain the defendant from disposing of his property,

(b) Appoint a receiver to take charge of the property,

(c) Set aside the conveyance or annul the obligation, or

(d) Make any order which the circumstances of the case may require.

Sec. 11. Cases Not Provided for in Act. In any case not provided for in the Act the rules of law and equity including the law merchant, and in particular the rules relating to the law of principal and agent, and the effect of fraud, misrepresentation, duress or coercion, mistake, bankruptcy or other invalidating cause shall govern.

Sec. 12. Construction of Act. This Act shall be so interpreted and construed as to effectuate its general purpose to make uniform the law of those states which enact it.

Sec. 13. Name of Act. This Act may be cited as the Uniform Fraudulent Conveyance Act.

Sec. 14. Inconsistent Legislation Repealed. Section ...... are hereby repealed, and all acts or parts of acts inconsistent with this Act are hereby repealed.

FINANCIAL INVENTORY FORMS

Net Worth Statement

Net Worth Of _____ as of _____

Assets:

Cash on Hand	$_____
Bank Accounts (all checking and savings)	$_____
Other Savings (C.D.s, Credit Union Accts., etc.)	$_____
House (market value)	$_____
Other Real Estate (market value)	$_____
Household Furnishings (market value)	$_____
Automobile(s) (blue book value)	$_____
Life Insurance (cash value)	$_____
Stocks, Bonds (current value)	$_____
Profit-Sharing or Retirement Plans	$_____
Other Assets (not previously listed)	$_____
TOTAL ASSETS	$_____

Debts:

Mortgages (balance due)	$_____
Installment Loans (balance due)	$_____
Other Loans (balance due)	$_____
Credit Cards (balance due)	$_____
Charge Accounts (amount owed)	$_____
Other Loans (not previously mentioned)	$_____
Insurance Premiums Due	$_____
Taxes Owed to Date	$_____
TOTAL DEBTS	$_____
NET WORTH (Total Assets Minus Total Debts)	$_____

Home Ownership Data

Property At_____

Purchase Date: _____   Purchase Price: $ _____   Principal: $ _____

Interest Rate:_____   Mortgage Term:_____   Assumable: ❏ Yes   ❏ No

Mortgage: _____

Address:_____

City: _____   State: _____   Zip:_____   Phone:_____

Holder of Contract For Deed: _____

Contract Amount: $ _____   Term of Contract:_____

Interest Rate:_____   Due: _____

Other Terms:_____

_____

_____

Address:_____

City: _____   State: _____   Zip:_____   Phone:_____

Most Recent Assessed Value: $ _____   Date: _____

Location of Deed: _____

Register number (Deed): _____

Property Tax Records Location: _____

Additional Information: _____

_____

_____

_____

_____

_____

_____

Home Inventory

Item	Purchased From	Date Purchased	Price
_____	_____	_____	$_____
_____	_____	_____	$_____
_____	_____	_____	$_____
_____	_____	_____	$_____
_____	_____	_____	$_____
_____	_____	_____	$_____
_____	_____	_____	$_____
_____	_____	_____	$_____
_____	_____	_____	$_____
_____	_____	_____	$_____
_____	_____	_____	$_____
_____	_____	_____	$_____
_____	_____	_____	$_____
_____	_____	_____	$_____
_____	_____	_____	$_____
_____	_____	_____	$_____
_____	_____	_____	$_____
_____	_____	_____	$_____
_____	_____	_____	$_____
_____	_____	_____	$_____
_____	_____	_____	$_____
_____	_____	_____	$_____
_____	_____	_____	$_____
_____	_____	_____	$_____
_____	_____	_____	$_____
_____	_____	_____	$_____

Bank Accounts

Bank _____

Branch Address: _____

Savings Acct. No.: _____ Checking Acct. No.: _____

Authorized Signatures: _____

_____

Bank _____

Branch Address: _____

Savings Acct. No.: _____ Checking Acct. No.: _____

Authorized Signatures: _____

_____

Bank _____

Branch Address: _____

Savings Acct. No.: _____ Checking Acct. No.: _____

Authorized Signatures: _____

_____

Bank _____

Branch Address: _____

Savings Acct. No.: _____ Checking Acct. No.: _____

Authorized Signatures: _____

_____

Bank _____

Branch Address: _____

Savings Acct. No.: _____ Checking Acct. No.: _____

Authorized Signatures: _____

_____

Certificates of Deposit

Name _____

   Trustee: _____

   Certificate of Deposit Account Number:_____

   Principal: $:_____   Interest Rate:_____   Maturity Date: _____

   Institution:_____

   Address:_____

   City: _____   State:_____   Zip: _____   Phone:_____

   Location of Certificate/Book: _____

   _____

   Additional Information: _____

   _____

   _____

   _____

Name _____

   Trustee: _____

   Certificate of Deposit Account Number:_____

   Principal: $:_____   Interest Rate:_____   Maturity Date: _____

   Institution:_____

   Address:_____

   City: _____   State:_____   Zip: _____   Phone:_____

   Location of Certificate/Book: _____

   _____

   Additional Information: _____

   _____

   _____

   _____

Money Market Funds

Name of Fund _____

    Account No.:_____   Amount Invested: $ _____

    As of (date):_____   Balance is: $ _____

    Certificate of Deposit Account Number:_____

    Firm: _____

    Account Supervisor: _____

    Address:_____

    City: _____   State:_____   Zip: _____   Phone:_____

    Location of Documentation: _____

    _____

    Additional Information: _____

    _____

    _____

Name of Fund _____

    Account No.:_____   Amount Invested: $ _____

    As of (date):_____   Balance is: $ _____

    Certificate of Deposit Account Number:_____

    Firm: _____

    Account Supervisor: _____

    Address:_____

    City: _____   State:_____   Zip: _____   Phone:_____

    Location of Documentation: _____

    _____

    Additional Information: _____

    _____

    _____

Investment Securities

Security Listing	No. Shares	Date Acquired	Maturity Date	Cost Price
				$
				$
				$
				$
				$
				$
				$
				$
				$
				$
				$
				$
				$
				$
				$
				$
				$
				$
				$
				$
				$
				$
				$
				$
				$
				$
				$

Savings Bonds

Name(s): _____

Bond Number	Face Value	Issue Date	Location of Bond
_____	$_____	_____	_____
_____	$_____	_____	_____
_____	$_____	_____	_____
_____	$_____	_____	_____
_____	$_____	_____	_____
_____	$_____	_____	_____
_____	$_____	_____	_____
_____	$_____	_____	_____
_____	$_____	_____	_____
_____	$_____	_____	_____
_____	$_____	_____	_____
_____	$_____	_____	_____
_____	$_____	_____	_____
_____	$_____	_____	_____
_____	$_____	_____	_____
_____	$_____	_____	_____
_____	$_____	_____	_____
_____	$_____	_____	_____
_____	$_____	_____	_____
_____	$_____	_____	_____
_____	$_____	_____	_____
_____	$_____	_____	_____
_____	$_____	_____	_____
_____	$_____	_____	_____
_____	$_____		

Keoghs and IRAs

Individual _____

Type of Plan: _____ Account Number: _____

   Periodic Investment: $ _____ per _____ Date Opened: _____

   Where Invested: _____

   Account Supervisor: _____

   Address: _____

   City: _____ State: _____ Zip: _____ Phone: _____

   Trustee/Beneficiary: _____

   Location of Documentation: _____

   _____

   Additional Information: _____

   _____

   Balance as of: _____ $ _____

Type of Plan: _____ Account Number: _____

   Periodic Investment: $ _____ per _____ Date Opened: _____

   Where Invested: _____

   Account Supervisor: _____

   Address: _____

   City: _____ State: _____ Zip: _____ Phone: _____

   Trustee/Beneficiary: _____

   Location of Documentation: _____

   _____

   Additional Information: _____

   _____

   Balance as of: _____ $ _____

Benefit Plans

Name: _____   **Date:** _____

Employer: _____   **Contact:** _____

Address: _____   **Phone:** _____

Location of Benefit Plan: _____

Benefits available as of above date:

Deferred Compensation $ _____

Group Life Insurance $ _____

Post-Death Salary Compensation $ _____

Stock Options $ _____

Restricted Stock $ _____

Pension Plan Contribution $ _____

Vested Employer's Contribution $ _____

Profit-Sharing Plan Contribution $ _____

Savings Plan Contribution $ _____

Vested Employee's Contribution $ _____

Other Benefit Plans $ _____

Collectibles

Inventory of Jewelry, Art, Heirlooms, Antiques, etc.

Item	Date Purchased	Purchace Price	Current Value

Deposit Box Inventory

Date of Record: _____

Location of Safety Deposit Box: _____

Address: _____

City: _____   State: _____   Zip: _____   Phone: _____

Trustee/Beneficiary: _____

Number: _____   Location of Key: _____

Owners/Keyholders: _____

_____

Inventory of Items:

Description   **Appraisal or Estimated Value**

_____   _____

_____   _____

_____   _____

_____   _____

_____   _____

_____   _____

_____   _____

_____   _____

_____   _____

_____   _____

_____   _____

_____   _____

_____   _____

_____   _____

_____   _____

_____   _____

Business Interests

Individual _____ **Date:** _____

Business Name: _____

    Address:_____

    Ownership Interest: _____

    _____

    Amount Paid: $_____   Present Value: $ _____

    Evidence of Ownership:_____

    _____

Business Name: _____

    Address:_____

    Ownership Interest: _____

    _____

    Amount Paid: $_____   Present Value: $ _____

    Evidence of Ownership:_____

    _____

Business Name: _____

    Address:_____

    Ownership Interest: _____

    _____

    Amount Paid: $_____   Present Value: $ _____

    Evidence of Ownership:_____

    _____

Copyrights and Patents

Name_____

Name or Description of Copyright or Patent_____

_____

    Issued By:_____   Date _____

    Identification Number: _____

    Additional Information: _____

    _____

Name or Description of Copyright or Patent_____

_____

    Issued By:_____   Date _____

    Identification Number: _____

    Additional Information: _____

    _____

Name or Description of Copyright or Patent_____

_____

    Issued By:_____   Date _____

    Identification Number: _____

    Additional Information: _____

    _____

Name or Description of Copyright or Patent_____

_____

    Issued By:_____   Date _____

    Identification Number: _____

    Additional Information: _____

    _____

Boats/Planes

Owned By: _____

Make: _____ Model: _____

Length: _____ Engine: _____

Other Description: _____

_____

_____

_____

_____

Identification Number: _____ Registration: _____

Date Purchased: _____ Price: $ _____

Purchased From: _____

_____

Docked/Stored At: _____

_____

Insured By: _____

Insured Value: $ _____ Liability: $ _____

Additional information: _____

_____

_____

_____

_____

_____

_____

_____

_____

_____

_____

Other Assets

Asset: _____

    Description:_____

    _____

    Purchase Date: _____   Gross Price: $ _____   Date Sold: _____

    Present Value: $ _____   Model:_____

    _____

    Additional Information: _____

    _____

Asset: _____

    Description:_____

    _____

    Purchase Date: _____   Gross Price: $ _____   Date Sold: _____

    Present Value: $ _____   Model:_____

    _____

    Additional Information: _____

    _____

Asset: _____

    Description:_____

    _____

    Purchase Date: _____   Gross Price: $ _____   Date Sold: _____

    Present Value: $ _____   Model:_____

    _____

    Additional Information: _____

    _____

Debtor Protection Strategies 3

Consumer credit agencies and insolvency attorneys report that most people who lose personal assets to creditor claims are those who have a number of pressing debts. Although it is possible that a financial catastrophe will take the form of one big lawsuit or some other single disaster, the odds are that there will be competing creditors, each in a race to be first to have their claims satisfied *before* you lose your property to other creditors.

If you are in serious financial difficulty, you may be experiencing extreme creditor pressure. Creditors may be threatening you with lawsuits, or harassing you with phone calls, or perhaps even garnishing your wages.

As an early step in your asset protection program you must know how to protect yourself from creditors. This protection should provide you with a long-term debt workout that can be set in motion at a reasonable pace. Your goal in structuring this strategy should be to eliminate the threatened loss of your personal assets or to buy the time needed to put your asset protection plan into effect.

How Creditors Collect

To best understand the self-protection strategies outlined in this chapter, you should understand how creditors try to collect on their overdue accounts.

It should make you feel somewhat better to realize that creditors are businesspeople and businesspeople always try to preserve goodwill, so that they do not damage the efforts of their sales department. So, creditors will give you the benefit of the doubt as long as they feel you eventually will pay. Customer retention is vitally important to their own success.

Collectors must also collect economically. Collection departments can become expensive. Therefore, much pressure is put on them to expend as little money as possible in collecting overdue accounts, and not to waste money on small, hard-to-collect accounts.

Between creditors wanting to preserve goodwill, while directing their strongest efforts on larger or easy-to-collect accounts, you probably have more negotiating strength than you thought possible if you owe relatively small amounts.

Collecting of overdue accounts is divided into different steps. Each step varies in its pressure in coaxing you to pay. Specific steps will, of course, vary greatly among different creditors.

Generally, the first step in handling an overdue account is a reminder notice. This gentle notification, usually found on your statement, or sometimes mailed separately, reminds you that your account is past due. The creditor assumes you have either overlooked the bill or are temporarily low on funds and that this notification will remind you to pay. Past due reminders are designed so they neither offend nor make the debtor feel guilty for being tardy. Most overdue accounts do pay at this point, and still others pay after a second reminder.

Professional credit departments realize the importance of speed when an account falls behind. It has been proven again and again that the longer a creditor waits, the less chance there is for payment. Therefore, good collection departments send a reminder letter 10 days after the due date with follow-ups, 20 days, or 30 days later. This barrage of reminders frequently works, as it keeps the bill foremost in the debtor's mind while he decides which bills to pay. The debtor well realizes that this creditor has not forgotten his account.

The next step is usually an "Is there anything wrong?" type letter or phone call.

Form letters are popular but the phone is becoming the preferred method of communication, especially as a follow-up to a letter reminder.

Credit card companies prefer telephone collections because of its speed. Fast action is important to them so they can quickly determine whether they should cancel the card. Time is money in this instance.

Although creditors realize deadbeats exist they are still likely to give the benefit of the doubt to the debtor and hope that an appeal to his better nature will encourage payment. The creditor will seek to learn the reasons for nonpayment and determine whether the debtor can be expected to pay, i.e., the probability of payment without legal action.

At this stage, delinquent customers become nothing more than overdue accounts to be collected without consideration for any future business they might bring. In fact, creditors may no longer want you as a customer because you are costing them too much money. On the other hand, you may be able to redeem your customer status by paying the account or making arrangements. However, expect to be watched closely in the future should the creditor decide to trust you with credit.

How Collection Agencies Collect

Once your account is turned over to a collection agency, you'll receive a brief notice informing you that your account has been referred to the agency for collection. The notice states the amount owed, the name of the creditor and asks you to contact the agency. This first letter is usually mild and unthreatening. It is surprising how much money agencies do collect from this first notice. Collection agencies have a reputation that convinces many people to pay who could have as readily paid the creditor directly but did not do so for any number of reasons.

After your first notice, the agency starts a barrage of letters and phone calls, all

basically with the same message, but increasingly tougher in tone and trickier as they go along. Once collectors make certain demands and you still fail to pay, they become increasingly stern on the next communication. Expect credit agencies to become more forward, more urgent, or more legal-sounding as you continue to resist payment.

Collection policies do vary. Some agencies, for example, send debtors a second notice. This probably mentions that there is a claim against you and that they intend to collect. Other agencies go directly into "final demands" and "final notices" and "final notices before suit." They may also try frequent phone calls. The telephone is a favorite collection tool because statements can be made by telephone that wouldn't be legally safe on paper. The telephone is also more intimidating. Once final demands are made, legal action may be imminent. So it is basically a choice of style and question of time, until collectors either give up or send the account to lawsuit.

Collectors make great effort to assure you that they are committed to collection. Their letters appear quite legal though they are not actual legal documents. Letters that appear as a legal document are frowned upon by most state codes regulating collection agencies, and by strict federal laws. Some agencies still use them, since letters are cheaper than filing suit. Yet "final notice before suit" letters that you receive don't necessarily mean what they say. What they do mean is that your account may now be sent to a lawyer for handling. The lawyer may feel the collector's notice was sufficient warning, though you will usually receive at least one or two collection letters from the lawyer. Once the lawyer has made a final but futile plea before suit, legal action will begin providing collection efforts which are believed worthwhile.

You can frequently convince a lawyer to settle for a very small percentage of the debt because most lawyers understandably want to avoid a time-consuming suit on a small claim. In many instances, a lawyer has no actual intention of suing but, like the collection agency, only hopes his letters will bring results.

Should you be sued it is time to call in your own attorney (unless it is a small claims case). Do not ignore the lawsuit. It can only bring about a default judgement that you will want to avoid.

Protecting Yourself Against Unlawful Collection Techniques

Considering the wide array of legitimate collection techniques available to collection agencies, it is surprising how many continue to resort to illegal, harassing conduct to collect for their clients. But you can effectively protect yourself once you know your rights!

Third party collection agencies and attorneys retained to collect debts are regulated by the Fair Debt Collection Practices Act, passed by Congress in 1978. This act specifically outlines what a debt collector is prohibited from doing when collecting debts for others. Unfortunately, creditors themselves are not covered by the act, nor are commercial debts owed by businesspeople.

A debt collector *may not*:

- Contact you at inconvenient or unusual times or places, such as before 8 a.m. or after 9 p.m.

- Contact you at your place of work.

- Contact you after you send written notice to the agency to stop, except to say that there will be no further contact, or to notify you that a specific action shall be taken if that specific action is, in fact, usually done by the collector.

- Contact anyone but your attorney, if you have one. Otherwise a collector may contact other people only to discover where you live or work.

- Tell people—other than you or your attorney—that you owe money.

- Advertise your debt, or publish a list of non-payers (except to credit bureaus).

- Harass, oppress, or abuse any person; or use threats of violence or harm to property or reputation, use obscene or profane language, repeatedly use the telephone to annoy, or telephone without identifying themselves.

- Make false statements when collecting a debt, such as: falsely implying that they are attorneys or government representatives, falsely imply that you have committed a crime, falsely implying that they work for a credit bureau, misrepresent the amount of debt, indicate papers are legal when they are not, or vice versa.

- Fail to give you written notice, within 5 days after first contacting you, telling you the amount owed, the name of the creditor, and what to do if you feel you do not owe the money.

- Contact you about the debt if you deny owing the debt within 30 days after being contacted, unless you are sent proof of the debt.

- Imply or say that you will be arrested for non-payments.

- Say that they will take legal action unless the creditor intends to do so and such action is legal.

- Give false credit information about you to anyone.

- Send you official-looking documents that appear like documents a court or agency of any United States government body might send.

- Use any false name.

- Deposit a post-dated check before the date on the check.

- Make you pay for communications such as collect calls or telegrams.

- Contact you by postcard.

- Put anything on an envelope that shows the communication is about the collection of a debt.

- Fail to apply any amounts to the specific debts you choose.

Threatening or actually writing complaint letters to regulatory agencies can have a calming effect on over-aggressive collectors. Creditors and collection agencies often do things that are illegal or are frowned upon by agencies such as the Federal Trade Commission (FTC), the post office, and the telephone company (which is regulated by the Federal Communications Commission),

but it is for you to know and assert your rights.

Once you discover that a collector has indeed broken a law, inform him the next time he contacts you that you are aware of his illegal activities and that you will contact the proper authorities if any illegality recurs. The threat of being reported usually will not prevent further attempts to collect, but it may considerably cool enthusiasm.

Complaints to the phone company against bill collectors are probably the closest you'll come to counter-intimidation. To collectors, the possibility of having their phone service disconnected is too dangerous. Much of their business of bill collecting is, of course, by telephone.

Should you have a legitimate complaint against a collection agency or attorney, then by all means contact your phone company. A complaint can be lodged if you are being harassed, threatened, called during the hours 9 p.m. to 7 a.m., called repeatedly during the same day, or called after you specifically said not to call again.

Your mere threat of complaint or actual complaint about misdeeds are just another barrier to collection you can effectively use. Each new barrier makes attempted collection on the account that much less worthwhile because collection efforts start to cost more than the amount owed. Remember these key points:

1. Creditors do not want to chase you on your delinquent bills. If you cannot pay immediately, notify your creditor as soon as possible. This "good faith" on your part will help you avoid aggravating collection efforts.

2. Collection agencies can do no more to you than can a creditor. In fact, a creditor is hampered in his collection efforts by severe federal laws.

3. You can fight back if you are unduly harassed by a creditor or collection agency. Know your rights and use them!

How To Solve Debt Problems Without Bankruptcy

Perhaps it seems your debts are so large you cannot possibly pay them and still put food on the table. You may simultaneously be threatened with:

1. Deductions from your wages (called "garnishment").

2. Loss of a purchased item to the seller (called "repossession").

3. Loss of your real estate (called "foreclosure").

4. Extreme bill collection measures such as late-night telephone calls from a collection agency (called "harassment").

5. Threats of creditors getting together to divide up all your available assets

(called "involuntary bankruptcy").

Clearly, you must do something decisive to solve your financial problems, but what can be done, short of declaring bankruptcy?

In fact, there are many ways to solve problems such as these, and often they can be solved with creditors in an amicable way — without bankruptcy — and you may even be able to preserve your good credit rating while you do so.

Three of the debt-solving strategies we will discuss include:

1. Debt Consolidation Borrowing

2. Debt Installment Plans

3. Out of Court Settlements

Choose the Debt-Solving Remedy Right for You

First you must objectively understand when each of these three debt-reducing strategies can work, although it is possible to combine the features of each into your own tailor-made debt-solving program. For example, you may raise some cash through borrowing and at the same time ask creditors to accept as full settlement a fraction of what is owed. Similarly, creditors may be willing to extend payments towards either a compromised amount or the full amount due.

How can you determine which debt-reducing method is best for you?

Step 1. Determine Your Borrowing Power

Add up your cash and the amount you can reasonably borrow against your assets. If the total cash availability exceeds your debts, then a debt consolidation loan is all that is required, provided you can keep future expenses within your budget. Use the convenient "Asset Borrowing Chart" found at the end of this chapter to help calculate your true borrowing power.

Step 2. Determine Your Income Power

First, write down your annual take-home income after deductions (for taxes, etc.). Divide by 12 to get your monthly take-home income.

Second, itemize expenses that occur less than once a month and compute the monthly set-aside amount for those expenses. For instance, car insurance may be due once a year, in January. Therefore, divide payment by the number of months between now and January to obtain a monthly "set-aside" amount to insure sufficient funds to pay the insurance when it comes due. For example, if you need $200 in January and it's now March, you have 10 months to save. $200 divided by 10 months is $20 per month. Subtract this monthly set-aside amount from your monthly take-home income.

Next, list your monthly fixed expenses. These are basic living expenses which remain constant over the year. Include rent, gasoline and car or transportation costs, heating, utilities, food, rent or mortgage (including a second mortgage), real estate taxes, insurance, contributions, savings, clothing, tuition, child care, child support, telephone, entertainment, laundry and cleaning. Subtract these expenses from the remaining monthly take-home income.

Now you can calculate your monthly variable expenses. These include debts such as charge card loans, bank loans (other than mortgages), credit card payments, appliance payments, medical bills, dental bills, and other catch-all items such as old utility bills, etc. Ideally these "other debts" should not exceed 15-20% of your disposable take-home pay (after subtracting your housing costs). Subtract this from the left-over monthly take-home pay.

Do you have money left? If so, this is your "optional spending amount" which you can use to repay loans, credit cards, and other existing debts. If you show a negative amount because you are spending more than you are making, then you must consider the other options that can help lead you out of debt difficulties, such as debt consolidation or extension agreements with creditors.

If you can reasonably pay past bills within 6 to 12 months, using a combination of borrowing power and income power, then you can likely solve your problems by reaching an agreement with creditors to simply extend your debt payments.

However, if you cannot meet past obligations over the next 12 months, you may require either an out-of-court settlement with creditors, a wage earner plan or a bankruptcy claim (discussed in later chapters), as it is unlikely you can repay your creditors in full.

Debt-Consolidation Borrowing

Although it sounds like a contradiction, borrowing to pay debts is a recommended way for many people to stretch their debt over a long pay-back period. This way, monthly payments become more manageable. But never borrow unless you are certain that borrowing will solve your debt problems once and for all. Although temporarily more comfortable, paying debts over a longer period of time through borrowing can be slow torture for some people. Think it out and review your other options before you borrow.

There are several ways to raise the money needed to pay creditors. Borrowing from friends, relatives, or the more familiar sources such as banks or credit unions are alternative sources. Turn to these sources first for consolidation loans since their interest rates are competitive. They may not ask for your home or car or other property as loan collateral, and they may have the most lenient credit terms.

Other borrowing sources exist, but may be less desirable due to frequently misleading lending tactics, higher interest, or less professional attention to your personal needs. Many unscrupulous lenders are anxious to exploit people in financial difficulty so check out your lender thoroughly.

Financial institutions which offer "debt consolidation," "debt reorganization," or "debt pooling" loans can be easily found. These firms charge exceptionally high interest, and undoubtedly will want you to pledge your home or car to insure you will indeed pay the loan (after all, you are in a "financial dilemma" when you go to see them!).

Some lenders offer to handle discussions or "settlements" with your creditors as well as give you a loan. They may charge up to $300 or more for an "installation fee" to "install" you in a repayment plan, under which their attorneys write your creditors for you. Other firms may charge 12 to 35% of the amount you owe. These firms must be thoroughly checked for honesty and reliability.

Should you decide to proceed with a debt-consolidation loan, it is always better to borrow from a friend or family member if you can. Explain your situation honestly. Show which creditors you will pay with the loan proceeds and what your budget will be during the pay-back period. Always offer a reasonable interest rate, even to friends and relatives.

Finance companies, of course, are not as desirable as family or friends. They charge very high interest rates and are seldom friendly if you are late with a payment. With this in mind, cautiously contact a finance company to see if you can obtain a consolidation loan. Before you sign, review the figures carefully. Are the monthly payments within reach? Make sure you don't agree to pay the finance company more than you are willing or capable of paying. You may decide that because the total finance charges are so much more than the debt owed that you would rather sell property, get another job, or generally struggle for awhile rather than pay a huge loan. Read the fine print in the contract to see what the lender can do should you miss a payment, etc. You may feel that the finance company or lender has too much control over your assets, which is generally the case. Think this over carefully. Borrowing is seldom a panacea. It will only extend your pay-back period so the monthly payments are less, but by doing so the interest you pay will also increase.

Second or third mortgages or trust deeds or home equity loans have become an important loan source for many people. Finance companies are handling most second mortgages. Second mortgages for consolidation loans are increasingly common for several reasons. 1) The dramatic rise in home prices has given many people a huge equity in their home. 2) A home offers good collateral to secure loans. 3) Lower interest rates can be offered on a home loan compared to an unsecured loan.

Other ways of obtaining money to pay debts include refinancing your home mortgage or borrowing against life insurance. By taking advantage of the built-up equity in your home, or lower interest rates on new mortgages, you may sufficiently lower your monthly payments to allow you to cover your excess obligations. Borrowing against your life insurance policy has the drawback of leaving you uncovered if the loan is not repaid. Yet, if you are seriously in debt, this

option may be worthwhile.

Borrowing against your assets is only one way to raise cash to pay creditors. Consider instead whether you should sell some assets to pay your debts. Look objectively and carefully at the items you own. Items that aren't absolutely vital, or that you can no longer afford, are candidates for the sale.

When choosing what to sell, take several factors into consideration. First, what you sell should ideally have a high resale value compared to its retail price. Electronics and high quality art work or collections often do well. This is balanced against how badly you want to keep specific items. For example, you may want to sell your books but keep your stereo, even though the books won't bring as much compared to what you paid for them. Be objective when balancing personal wants against financial needs.

Some people get upset when they sell an item and the price doesn't come close to covering its cost. But don't let this discourage you from selling the item. If you don't need it, there is no use in keeping it just because you can only sell at a loss. Next time, make sure you look at the second-hand market before you splurge on that shiny new model which may have added to your financial difficulties in the first place.

Selling items you don't absolutely need will help you get out of debt that much faster. Sometimes it can take out a substantial chunk of debt, and that allows you to start buying things you really want that much sooner.

If you should return an item to a creditor, such as a car or refrigerator, make sure you get a *release* from the dealer. Otherwise, the dealer may come after you for a *deficiency judgement,* if the used item cannot be sold for enough to cover your outstanding loan. If you can't negotiate a release, then you probably should sell the item yourself. Even though you may not get enough to fully pay the loan, you may obtain more than the dealer who sells the items on distress sale.

Selling assets for the most money and

with the least trouble can be a very educational experience. There are many ways to sell assets for cash. You can advertise in local newspapers or classified listings, or you can make up cards and place them on public bulletin boards around work, supermarkets, post offices, schools, and universities. You can sell many items at yard sales, garage sales, or auctions. But you must sell aggressively because time is not on your side.

The sad truth is not many people learn their lessons even when they get a consoli-dation loan or sell assets. These individuals experience "freedom from debt" for perhaps a year, then are right up to their necks again in monthly payments — just like before! This time, they have few options because they are already burdened with a debt consolidation loan to solve earlier problems. Freedom from debt comes when you create a budget, live within the budget, and improve your life by feeling better about yourself because you do manage your money more intelligently.

Negotiate an Installment Plan

What if you have done your best to look for extra income, sold property to pay debts, and even borrowed to stretch out the debt? What is left to relieve your crushing debts? Bankruptcy? As long as you have some form of steady income you do not yet need to con-template bankruptcy. You need only threaten it. Installment plans work because creditors realize your option is probably bankruptcy, and unless you have substantial property, creditors will get little or nothing. Half a loaf is better than a crumb is the selling point you must use on creditors.

There are three basic ways installment plans can be administered. Each creates its own level of pressure for the creditor to ac-cept the plan. This is important because any plan requires a majority of creditors to agree to it.

The first level is a self-run program. You directly contact your creditors with your plan and hope that the threat of bankruptcy and their belief in your sincerity convinces them to accept your long-term payment proposal.

The second level is administered by a credit counselor, usually from a consumer credit counselling service in your area. Creditors are more apt to accept a plan sponsored by these organizations because creditors know you are in the hands of a professional organization which will make every possible effort to pay creditors punc-tually and equitably.

The third level (discussed later) is the court-administered installment plan referred to as the *Wage Earner's Plan*.

Once rejected by consolidation loan lenders, or should you feel more debt is not for you, use the following procedure. It is straightforward and simple. First, draft a letter to each of your creditors explaining your financial problem. Request a temporary reduction of payments until your financial affairs are again in order. (See the sample letters at the end of this chapter.) Advise creditors you intend to pay the entire amount owed. You are now asking all your creditors for patience and willingness to take reduced payments over a longer period of time.

Here is an example. Assume your in-come is $1,400 per month and your living expenses come to $1,200 per month. You thus have only $200 to pay towards monthly loans, which requires $400 per month. The $200 is available for your personal "consolidation payment" program. Since your current loan payments total $400 but you have only $200, or one half of the needed amount, offer each creditor one half of your normal payments. Keep a record of your payments and what you owe on the chart included in this chapter to help you keep records.

In a typical installment plan, you will submit to creditors a list of debts, a budget, and a proposed pay-back plan. First prepare a budget. It should be simple yet cover ev-erything you must spend. Consider that creditors will look closely at your budget and decide whether or not to accept your plan largely on whether they think you have made enough personal sacrifice. Remember, creditors will expect that you should be making a standard of living adjustment or they won't consider you very sincere. It is also worthwhile to remember no matter what you do, you have incurred debts, and will somehow pay for it. If the payment doesn't take the form of straight cash, then it will show up in the form of a lowered standard of living, loss of credit accessibility, loss of property, harassment from collectors, worry about the debt, or loss of pride. You can, however, help redeem yourself with creditors with a "bare bones" budget. Figure your income, subtract your budgeted expenses and the difference is what is available for creditors. Divide this amount among your creditors proportionate to the amount that you owe each one. Do not favor one creditor over another but treat each equally on a pro-rata basis. This, of course, applies only to general unsecured debts. Obligations such as real estate mortgages, car installment loans, taxes, alimony and support payments have priority and must be paid in full and in a manner different from the plan proposed to general creditors.

Here are four additional tips to follow:

1. Make the plan conditional upon acceptance by a majority of your creditors (usually creditors owed at least 90% of your debt).

2. Withhold all payments until you receive the necessary creditor agreements. It makes no sense to pay creditors piecemeal unless you are certain the entire plan is successful.

3. Secured creditors may decide they would rather repossess the item than rely upon your payment plan. Demand a signed statement that the creditor won't slap you for a deficiency judgement. Other creditors may tell you they will agree to your plan provided you sign a *confession of judgement*. Advise them you won't surrender your constitutional right to trial in the event a collection suit is brought.

4. Most importantly—make certain your agreements with creditors are in writing. Use the model forms contained in this chapter, or settlement agreements drafted by your own attorney.

Compromise Settlements

Besides debt-consolidation borrowing and extended payment plans, there is one other major method of settling your debt to a creditor and one which is a compromise settlement. This is often called a "composition agreement." It works primarily due to the threat of bankruptcy as the only other alternative. Creditors realize there are obvious advantages to a partial payment now rather than taking you to court or risking a bankruptcy where creditors may get little or nothing. But, for an out of court settlement to work you need to convince your creditors that you have little income and of greater importance, negligible assets. These realities show creditors that if you filed for bankruptcy, they would get nothing, or at least far less than you are offering. If you are sued, creditors would have a hard time collecting anything on their judgement, and probably not even recover their attorney's fees. This is the backdrop against which you must negotiate a compromise settlement.

The types of deals and settlement agreements available to you are as variable as your needs. Compromise settlements are actual contracts agreed upon and signed by both parties, the debtor and the creditor. As with any agreement, neither party will sign unless a benefit comes from doing so. When negotiating, remember to put yourself in the creditor's shoes, i.e., try to "read their minds." See what you can do to make creditors feel as good about the situation as possible. Most often, creditors will be anxious to get this collection problem off their backs quickly. They are probably tired of the situation too. In such cases, your strategy should be to gather as much money as possible and offer creditors a percentage of the debt owed in full settlement (such as 20% or 30%), payable immediately. With more patient creditors, you might work out deals under which higher percentages are paid back but not immediately. Payments can be due after a grace period of months or even years. It could be part cash now and the balance paid to the creditor in post-dated checks in installments. If you use post-dated checks, clearly write "POST-DATED CHECK" on the front of the check. This helps prevent it from being cashed too soon. Make certain to have the funds in your account when the check is due.

Be flexible with compromise settlements. Design a plan that makes sense for your situation. Take into consideration both your net worth and your income so you can show creditors your offer is fair.

When you use compromise settlements to resolve problems with all your creditors, you must obtain the agreement of at least a majority of the creditors. They must agree to the specific percentage you have set. Your contract is binding only on assenting creditors. You can prepare these offers yourself or you can use the help of a credit counselor or lawyer. See the model letter at the end of this chapter. Use it as a guideline for a typical letter and what it may include.

As with extension or installment agreements, your compromise settlement should be conditioned upon acceptance by a specified percentage of creditors and, of course, provide for equally proportionate payments to each creditor unless creditors have the option to select one of several different plans.

It is possible to negotiate a compromise settlement with one creditor when that creditor is owed most of the money and therefore represents your financial problem. Negotiations with one principal creditor are permissible, provided the creditor understands that other creditors are not being asked to compromise their debt.

Your Seven Point Negotiating Checklist

Reaching settlement with creditors is usually a matter of give and take.

You have your negotiating points, and the creditors have theirs. Creditors want as much money as possible and as soon as possible. With your survival instincts finely tuned, your goal is just the opposite.

As you do battle, keep this checklist at your fingertips. It includes every negotiating point that's bound to arise, plus the counterpoints you can effectively use against creditor demands:

1. How Much Will You Pay?

Start with 10% more than what creditors will likely receive under a bankruptcy. Increase your offer in increments of 5% if you must — but only after creditors grant even greater concessions. Don't forget attitude and negotiating strategies are essential to success.

2. How Much Now and How Much Later?

Offer as an immediate payment only what you can afford to pay. Future payments should never exceed more than what you safely calculate as surplus income.

3. Length of Payments

Creditors will try to get you to pay the entire amount, no matter how long it takes. Don't mortgage your future for more than one or two years. Convince creditors that it's just not worth it to you. Therefore, your total payment should never exceed the sum total of cash on hand plus surplus income for the following year or two.

4. What About Return Goods?

Merchandise or property that you can return for credit has a value equivalent to cash. You can use excess or unsalable inventory or property as a negotiating point, however, the return of property must be bartered the same as a cash payment.

5. *What About Interest on the Balance?*

If you propose a pay-out over time this point will certainly arise. Interest at the prime rate is reasonable, however, this too is a concession tool. Your best argument is to remind creditors that if you do go bankrupt, they may wait several years for their small dividend, and bankruptcy courts don't pay interest.

6. *Will the Creditor Give Up Putting a Negative Mark or Late Payment Code On Your Credit Rating?*

Your regularity and sincerity in repayment may influence creditors to decide that you deserve this consideration. Negotiate hard for it. This can be your one opportunity to preserve your credit rating.

7. *Offer Your Future Business.*

Your creditors may welcome prospects of future sales. Creditors willing to work cooperatively with you are deserving of your future business and they should be told of your own sincere belief in this policy.

Three Selling Points You Should Use

Here are the benefits to the creditor you must continually sell:

1. Your regular payments mean that creditors always know where you are. You are not "dropping out." Also, regular payments eliminate collection costs for special letters, phone calls and other actions. Regular, but low payments are better than irregular payments, or no payments at all.

2. Your sincerity, quick action and close contact with a creditor makes your relationship easy to maintain — especially compared to people who "skip out" from their debts, or are late without explanation. Point out to your creditor that although you are making smaller payments than initially required, you are nevertheless now making payments on time.

3. Your attempts to avoid bankruptcy offer creditors the big benefit of ultimately receiving a much greater payment than your bankruptcy would

yield. Under bankruptcy, your assets are divided up among your creditors according to the ratio of your assets to your total debts. For example, imagine that you owe a total of $100,000 and you have $20,000 in assets at liquidation. A bankruptcy court would direct that for every $10 of debt a creditor had against you, he would receive $2. Many times the ratio is $1 or less for every $10 owed. And there are many "no asset" bankruptcies where creditors receive absolutely nothing. Since individuals filing for bankruptcy seldom have significant assets, creditors would much prefer a plan where your future income is also directed towards discharging your debts.

For this reason, when creditors press for repayment of the entire amount, particularly if the amount is not secured by some kind of personal possession or property, they gladly listen to offers of slower repayment, or partial payments to satisfy their claim.

Where to Find Professional Assistance

Credit counselors can provide expert advice in arranging settlements with credi-

tors. There are three different types of credit counselors: Non-profit credit counselors, for-profit "pro-raters," and for-profit bill paying services. Always deal with non-profit counselors or for-profit bill paying services; forget the "pro-raters."

The non-profit counselors will first get the approval of all your creditors for a pay-back plan. Once that is accomplished, they ask the creditors for a donation (a 15% rebate) to support their activities. Most creditors pay because they realize that without the counselor's intervention they probably would not be paid at all. So, it is in the creditor's best interest to support these services. One drawback: do not expect to be granted further credit while using this type of service.

In contrast, pro-raters or debt poolers charge a percentage of your income off the top for the service they provide. Most often, though, they do not have the payment plan approved by the creditors first. This means that with their fee taken off the top, there is usually not enough left to pay what you owe and so your plan often falls apart as your creditors demand payment.

Bill paying services provide a superior type of payment plan for those who can afford it. Expect that all your past due payments will be brought up to date under a strict budget and thereafter will be paid precisely on the date due and for the amount that the payment plan calls for. This type of service has several advantages: it will help maintain your good credit standing and will permit you to expand your credit as needed. You will never suffer the stigma of having gone through a pro-rater payment plan. The better companies are fully computerized and perform their service with admirable efficiency.

To find the name of the nearest counseling agency in your area, write to the National Foundation For Consumer Credit, 1819 H Street, Washington D.C. 20006. This non-profit organization is most helpful. Or look in your yellow pages under credit counselors or financial planners. It will be listed as Consumer Credit Counselors of (your city). You can also try obtaining counseling through your place of work, credit union, bank, department store (credit department), your union, church, legal aid societies, or the army and navy. If you do use the counseling services of a bank or department store and you owe them any money, be aware that they will tend to pay themselves first at the expense of other creditors. An alternative but equally excellent referral agency is Family Service America, which has credit counseling services in approximately 40 cities. Assistance with marital and employment problems can be obtained as well. Contact them at:

Family Service America
11700 W. Lake Park Dr.
Milwaukee, WI   53224
(414) 359-2111

DEBTOR PROTECTION FORMS

Unpaid Debts

Owed By _____ As of _____

Owed To	Total Balance	Due Date	To Be Paid
_____	_____	_____	_____
_____	_____	_____	_____
_____	_____	_____	_____
_____	_____	_____	_____
_____	_____	_____	_____
_____	_____	_____	_____
_____	_____	_____	_____
_____	_____	_____	_____
_____	_____	_____	_____
_____	_____	_____	_____
_____	_____	_____	_____
_____	_____	_____	_____
_____	_____	_____	_____
_____	_____	_____	_____
_____	_____	_____	_____
_____	_____	_____	_____
_____	_____	_____	_____
_____	_____	_____	_____
_____	_____	_____	_____
_____	_____	_____	_____
_____	_____	_____	_____
_____	_____	_____	_____

Asset Borrowing Chart

Asset	Fair Market Value	Loan Value
	$ _____	$ _____
	$ _____	$ _____
	$ _____	$ _____
	$ _____	$ _____
	$ _____	$ _____
	$ _____	$ _____
	$ _____	$ _____
	$ _____	$ _____
	$ _____	$ _____
	$ _____	$ _____
	$ _____	$ _____
	$ _____	$ _____
	$ _____	$ _____
	$ _____	$ _____
	$ _____	$ _____
	$ _____	$ _____
	$ _____	$ _____
	$ _____	$ _____
	$ _____	$ _____
	$ _____	$ _____
	$ _____	$ _____
	$ _____	$ _____
	$ _____	$ _____
	$ _____	$ _____

Debt Liquidation Analysis

Month:

Food $_____

Rent/Mortgage $_____

Telephone $_____

Water & Power $_____

Electric/Gas $_____

Insurance

      Health $_____

      Auto $_____

      Homeowners $_____

Child Care $_____

Car Payments $_____

Gasoline $_____

Medical $_____

Other

_____ $_____

_____ $_____

_____ $_____

TOTAL $_____

Total Bare Necessities $_____

Minus After Tax Income $_____

= Monthly Amount Left Over For Debts $_____

Amount Left Over Or Amount Short $_____

Debt Consolidation Budget

Creditor	Balance Owed	Monthly Payment
_____	$ _____	$ _____
_____	$ _____	$ _____
_____	$ _____	$ _____
_____	$ _____	$ _____
_____	$ _____	$ _____
_____	$ _____	$ _____
_____	$ _____	$ _____
_____	$ _____	$ _____
_____	$ _____	$ _____
_____	$ _____	$ _____
_____	$ _____	$ _____
_____	$ _____	$ _____
_____	$ _____	$ _____
_____	$ _____	$ _____
_____	$ _____	$ _____
_____	$ _____	$ _____
_____	$ _____	$ _____
_____	$ _____	$ _____
_____	$ _____	$ _____
_____	$ _____	$ _____
_____	$ _____	$ _____
_____	$ _____	$ _____
_____	$ _____	$ _____
_____	$ _____	$ _____
_____	$ _____	$ _____

SAMPLE LETTER
TO REQUEST INSTALLMENT PAYMENTS

Ace Corporation
1000 Main Street
Anytown, USA 10001
Attn: Credit Manager

Dear Sir:

Due to recent unemployment and illness in the family, I have found it impossible to pay my debts as they fall due and therefore find it necessary to propose payment of my indebtedness to you in the amount of $1,200 in 24 monthly installments of $50 each.

I have attached my monthly budget which discloses I have only $400 available each month (after necessary living expenses) and this must be applied to my total indebtedness of approximately $10,000. Therefore, under my proposed plan each of my creditors shall receive an equally proportionate payment each month.

As you can understand, I have made a significant sacrifice in my living standard to arrange this payment plan. I am equally confident you share my view that your patience in receiving payment is far preferable to a forced bankruptcy that would yield little or nothing for creditors.

If this proposed installment plan is satisfactory, please sign and return one copy of this letter for my record. Payments will commence on the first day of the following month.

I appreciate your understanding and cooperation.

Sincerely,

John B. Smith
999 Central Street
Anytown, USA

Accepted:

_____
Creditor
Date:

SAMPLE LETTER FOR OUT-OF-COURT SETTLEMENT

Ace Corporation
1000 Main Street
Anytown, USA 10001
Attn: Credit Manager

Dear Sir:

Due to recent unemployment and illness in the family, I have found it impossible to pay my debts in full. My present income leaves nothing for back bills and I have no assets or personal possessions to either sell or borrow against.

Considering the extent of my total indebtedness, it will be impossible to pay them fully and therefore I am offering to pay creditors 25% on the dollar (in five installments of 5% each) in full settlement and satisfaction of the debt owed. This proposal is being made this date to all my creditors.

If this is acceptable to you, please sign one copy of this letter and return for my records.

I regret this action is necessary, however I am confident it will enable creditors to receive more than could be obtained under bankruptcy and therefore you will join with other creditors in accepting this plan.

Thank you for your cooperation.

Sincerely,

John B. Smith
999 Central Street
Anytown, USA

Accepted:

_____
Creditor
Date:

AGREEMENT TO EXTEND DEBT PAYMENT

FOR VALUE RECEIVED, the undersigned

        (Creditor) and   (Debtor)

hereby acknowledge and agree that:

1.   The Debtor presently owes the Creditor the sum of $, said sum being presently due and payable, but that Debtor is unable to fully pay same at present.

2.   In further consideration of the Creditor's forbearance, the Debtor agrees to pay said debt on extended terms in the manner following:

3.   In the event the Debtor fails to make any payments punctually on the agreed extended terms, the Creditor shall have full rights to proceed for the collection of the entire balance then remaining.

4.   In the event of default in payment the Debtor agrees to pay all reasonable attorneys' fees and costs of collection.

5.   This agreement shall be binding upon and inure to the benefit of the parties, their successors, assigns and personal representatives.

Signed under seal this   day of   , 19 .

_____
Creditor

_____
Debtor

AGREEMENT TO COMPROMISE DEBT

BE IT KNOWN, for good consideration, the undersigned as a creditor of

_____ (Debtor) hereby enters into this agreement to

compromise and discharge the indebtedness due from Debtor to the undersigned on the

following terms and conditions:

1.   The Debtor and the undersigned acknowledge that the present debt due and owing

creditor is in the amount of $

2.   The parties agree that the undersigned creditor shall accept the sum of $

as full and total payment on said debt and in complete discharge, release, satisfaction and

settlement of all monies presently due, provided the sum herein shall be fully and

punctually paid in the manner following:

3.   In the event the Debtor fails to fully and punctually pay the compromised amount,

the undersigned creditor shall have full rights to prosecute its claim for the full amount of

$ less credits for payments made.

4.   In the event of default in payment the Debtor agrees to pay all reasonable attorneys'

fees and costs of collection.

5.   This agreement shall be binding upon and inure to the benefit of the parties, their

successors, assigns and personal representatives.

Signed under seal this   day of   , 19   .

Witnesseth:

_____   _____
                                           Creditor

_____   _____
                                           Debtor

Creditor Payment Chart

Creditor: _____

Balance owed: $ _____   Amount agreed to be paid: $ _____

How Paid: _____

_____

_____

_____

_____

Payment Record

Creditor	Balance Owed	Monthly Payment
_____	$ _____	$ _____
_____	$ _____	$ _____
_____	$ _____	$ _____
_____	$ _____	$ _____
_____	$ _____	$ _____
_____	$ _____	$ _____
_____	$ _____	$ _____
_____	$ _____	$ _____
_____	$ _____	$ _____
_____	$ _____	$ _____
_____	$ _____	$ _____
_____	$ _____	$ _____
_____	$ _____	$ _____
_____	$ _____	$ _____
_____	$ _____	$ _____
_____	$ _____	$ _____
_____	$ _____	$ _____

GENERAL RELEASE

BE IT KNOWN, for good consideration, the undersigned hereby jointly and severally forever releases, discharges, acquits and forgives

from any and all claims, actions, suits, demands, agreements, liabilities and proceedings of every nature and description both at law and in equity arising from the beginning of time to the date of these presence and more particularly related to an incident or claim that arose out of:

This release shall be binding upon and inure to the benefit of the parties, their successors, assigns and personal representatives.

Signed under seal this   day of   , 19   .

Witnesseth:

_____   _____

_____   _____

Foreclosure, Repossession and Tax Seizure Avoidance 4

Unlike general or unsecured creditors, the bank or lender who holds a mortgage on your home or auto is an entirely different breed of creditor. And unlike creditors covered in the previous chapter, serious delinquency with a mortgage is not usually a simple matter of negotiation. More than anything else, the inability to meet monthly mortgage payments is the sign of *serious* indebtedness which can easily cause you to lose your property.

Banks and lenders do not enjoy foreclosing on a home or repossessing a car or boat. A "problem" loan is a reflection of the lenders own mistaken judgement.

Moreover, a foreclosure often creates poor public relations and may even yield the lender less proceeds than if he cooperated with the borrower and negotiated a sensible workout.

Still, a bank or lender holding an adequately secured mortgage against property must be reckoned with on terms satisfactory to the lender because your lender knows he can recoup his loan. Therefore any consideration is based on the borrower's own sincere efforts to bring the loan current, and commitment to work his/her way out of these difficulties.

How to Avoid Foreclosure

If you are behind on your mortgage payments by two to three months, or a lender has threatened or started foreclosure, it is probably a good idea to seek the services of a real estate lawyer. An experienced lawyer knows best how to negotiate with lenders and can often see solutions you may overlook or not know about.

There are, however, only so many

possibilities when facing a mortgage foreclosure. Consider these strategies:

1. *Sell the house:* If you have fallen behind on your mortgage payment simply because you can't afford the house, then sell the house as quickly as possible and down-size to a home you can afford. A sale is far better than a fore-

closure as it preserves equity and avoids an adverse credit report and costly foreclosure costs.

2. *Accept the lender as a partner:* If you can't afford the mortgage, the lender may accept a percentage of the equity in the property and in return, cancel part of the loan. This is particularly true if the property is rapidly appreciating in value.

3. *Equity-share with a third-party:* The lender may be unwilling to trade part of his loan for equity, however, it may be an attractive investment to some other investor. Shop around.

4. *Offer additional collateral:* Frequently a lender will forebear if offered additional collateral. This is particularly true when the loan balance is close to the value of the property and the lender is concerned whether he can recoup his loan from the property or believes he will lose more by delay.

5. *Prioritize:* Often mortgage delinquencies are caused by a borrower spending money on non-essentials instead of giving priority to such essentials as a home loan. If this is your situation, the solution is simply to reverse your priorities and pay the mortgage first. Mortgages and taxes should always be paid ahead of other creditors.

6. *Refinance:* You may be able to substantially reduce your monthly mortgage payments by refinancing. This is particularly so if you have a short-term or high-interest loan. What would your new payments be with a new lower interest, long-term loan?

7. *Obtain a second mortgage:* A second mortgage may be just the answer if you have equity in your property and have fallen behind on your first mortgage because of a temporary financial problem. The second mortgage can then be used to bring the first mortgage current.

8. *Borrow against other assets:* If you cannot borrow against your home, see if you can borrow against some other assets to catch up on your mortgage.

9. *Offer interest only:* If your problems are temporary, offer to pay interest only for three to six months (or until you can begin to bring the mortgage current). This may substantially lower your payments, particularly if you have an older mortgage where most of the payment is applied to interest.

10. *Offer a bonus:* If the lender is unwilling to settle for interest only then offer a few "points" as a bonus. Frequently this will be attractive to the lender, particularly when the present interest is low in relation to currently prevailing interest.

11. *Renegotiate interest:* If the present interest is substantially lower than prevailing rates, the lender is likely to be uncooperative upon a default as he prefers to "reinvest" his loan at a higher rate. In this instance it may be necessary to renegotiate a higher interest rate which, while costly, may nevertheless be more feasible than refinancing.

12. *Negotiate a payment moratorium:* A lender may agree to a total "hold" or moratorium on payments (principal and interest) if he believes there is adequate equity in the property and the moratorium does not exceed several months.

13. *Agree to a reduced term:* A lender may cooperate with a moratorium on principal and/or interest, if you agree to shorten the term of the note. For example, a twenty year note may be shortened to three or five years but with payments based on twenty years.

14. *Look for a co-signer:* If the lender's concern is the collateral value of the property, he may become more lenient with a co-signer on the loan. You may find a co-signer who sees a greater value in the property.

15. *Check the loan documents:* If the lender is uncooperative and insists upon foreclosure it is wise to have your loan documents checked by an attorney. There may be one or more violations of the numerous lending statutes and this may stop foreclosure or at least greatly improve your negotiating posture.

16. *Consider a Chapter 13 Wage Earner Plan:* One sure way to stop foreclosure when all else fails is to file a Wage Earner Plan (Chapter 13) in the Bankruptcy Court. A Chapter 13 will prevent foreclosure, although you will have to stay current on future payments. Any arrearage can be paid over the three year plan period, as further explained in the following chapter.

A Chapter 13 can also be used to reduce a loan balance to the value of the property and is an excellent remedy when you have an "over-financed" property.

How to Stop Repossession of Personal Property

Banks and finance companies employ similar types of collection tactics for delinquent loans on personal property. These lenders can be stalled for a short time, but become impatient quickly because: 1) They have interest in property which makes collection easier; and 2) They realize that the longer the account is delinquent, the harder it will be to collect later.

Because of the recent rise in bankruptcies, collection departments now stay on top of their accounts and quickly push for payment when danger signals arise. They often subscribe to "early warning" systems from credit bureaus. Should you become delinquent to one creditor and it is reported to the credit bureau, your name goes on a list that may be sent to some of your other creditors. Still, most secured lenders care little about your general credit but become concerned only when you fall behind on their specific loan.

With auto loans, there sometimes is the option of refinancing. Finance companies particularly welcome this. As long as they feel you have the ability to pay the new "low" monthly payment, they will refinance. But don't get stuck in the trap of constant refinancing. Use it to bail out only in case of an emergency.

Tip:

Beware if you're past due on a bank loan and have a bank or checking account with them.

Banks usually have a clause in the loan contract allowing them to automatically collect the amount due from your account which they usually do after a couple of months of non-payment.

As with other lenders, banks and finance companies hesitate to go to court or seize assets. Communicate with them, show that you have a sincere willingness to pay, and will soon be able to, and you can extend the time before they go to court for seizure or repossession of assets.

Most loans have clauses which makes the entire amount of the loan due and payable if a payment is missed. It also allows the bank or finance company to repossess a car, for example. Auto sales are fueled by easy credit. This causes problems because people are allowed to borrow even though they are unable to pay the loan. This means banks and finance companies must have fast, effective collection procedures. Collecting on auto loans is generally aggressive, and lenders will not hesitate to repossess your car or boat if you fail to pay, although they are understandably more lenient on foreclosing on a family home.

Many of the strategies that can be used to avoid a real estate foreclosure can be equally successful in preventing repossession of an auto, boat or other personal property, because in concept both types of lenders are in a similar position. So be willing to use the same negotiating techniques.

It is important to understand your rights in the event a repossession is threatened.

Repossessions are governed under the Uniform Commercial Code, which is applicable in all states. The Code states the following:

- A creditor may take possession of collateral on the default of the debtor, "if this can be done without a breach of the peace."

- In cases in which a debtor has paid 60 percent of the cash price of a purchase or of a loan for goods, the creditor must dispose of the collateral and return to the consumer any amount in excess of the debt and any reasonable expenses incurred by the creditor in the collection. If you owned a boat, for example, which you had paid for with a loan that was secured by the boat, and had paid 60 percent or more of the loan when the boat was repossessed, the creditor would have to sell the boat, and give you any "profit" he made from the sale — minus the "reasonable expenses" and what was owing at the time of the repossession.

- The debtor has the right, up to the time the creditor has disposed of the prop-

erty seized, to redeem the collateral by payment of the remaining debt plus expenses.

- The creditor must notify the debtor before disposing of the collateral.

Unfortunately, the debtor has very few rights that would guarantee that the repossessed property was sold at a reasonable price. Most autos that have been repossessed, for example, are sold at public auction, where the bids can be fairly low. If the money received in the resale does not equal the amount owed by the debtor, the creditor can go back to court for an execution after levy, basically a garnishment to recover the deficit on the debt.

You can fight what you feel is an unreasonable sale of repossessed property, but, to do so you must go to court and prove that the price received for the goods was "commercially unreasonable," and that the method of resale was unconscionable on the part of the creditor or repossessor. This is exceptionally difficult to establish in most cases.

If the creditor fails to comply with these rules, a consumer can seek an injunction to stop a sale, receive punitive damages if the collateral has already been disposed of, or obtain cancellation of any deficiency owed.

How to Deal With the IRS

You may owe the IRS money for a variety of reasons — your business failed and you owe withholding taxes, you were audited and came out with a large tax liability, or you simply owe taxes on your current tax return for which you do not have the money to pay.

By now you probably know just how far-reaching the IRS collection powers can be. After a series of collection notices the IRS can and will:

- File a tax lien which automatically encumbers any property in your name.

- Levy on a bank or savings account.

- Garnish wages.

- Seize and sell any property they can locate.

Therefore, a fundamental rule when you owe the IRS (or any other taxing authority) is to have as few assets in your name as possible.

It is also a good idea to keep your funds in a bank the IRS does not know about so it cannot be readily levied. For example, you should pay tax bills by money orders or funds drawn on another account, rather than on the account where your money is kept.

The Seizure Process

Seizures can be avoided through prompt communication with the IRS. The IRS will collect delinquent taxes without resorting to seizures, but only if you take the initiative and responsibility to explore available alternatives and to propose a payment arrangement compatible with your financial situation. Almost all IRS seizures can be avoided or prevented if taxpayers will either cooperate more fully or quickly communicate their problems to the IRS.

If the IRS has already sent you the computer notices and someone from the IRS is talking tough about enforced collection, do not despair. Payment arrangements are still possible at any time, even after a seizure has already been made. In fact, a large number of payment arrangements are made after a levy or a seizure. Many taxpayers do not take the IRS computer notices or phone calls seriously until it is too late.

IRS policy allows taxpayers a reasonable opportunity to pay voluntarily and comply with the tax laws before taking any seizure action. IRM 5311:(5) states that "before levy or seizure is taken on an account, the taxpayer should be informed, except in jeopardy situations, that levy or seizure will be the next action taken and given a reasonable opportunity to pay voluntarily. Once the taxpayer has been advised and neglects to make satisfactory arrangements, levy action should be taken expeditiously."

Code Section 6331(d) requires that a written notice be sent before making a seizure of your salary, wages or other property. The IRS' last computer notice, titled "Past Due Final Notice," serves as official notification of such possible seizure action. The last computer notice states that "enforcement action can be taken at any time after ten days . . . Bank accounts, receivables, commissions, and other income are also subject to levy. Property or rights to property, such as automobiles or boats, may also be seized and sold to satisfy your tax liability."

The Tax Code requires that the written notice either be given in person, left at your residence or usual place of business, or sent by certified or registered mail to your last known address. Sending the final notice to your last known address fulfills the written notification requirement, even if the notice is returned to the IRS as undeliverable. Consider the final notice your first serious warning.

The second warning usually comes a few weeks later via a phone call from the collection interviewer, who will probably try to put "the fear" into you by telling you that if you don't pay they will either send a Revenue Officer out to start seizing your assets or they may send out a levy notice to attach your paycheck or bank account. For many taxpayers this is the second but last, serious warning. At this point, though, immediate seizure activity will only be made on paychecks and bank accounts.

Seizures of other types of property, such as businesses, automobiles, and real estate, can only be made by Revenue Officers who are also required to warn you if they are contemplating any such seizure action. The warning from the Revenue Officer is your third and *final* serious warning.

As you can see, the warnings can occur at any stage of the collection process, either from the final notice, subsequent phone calls, or the collection interview.

Tip:

Any warning of seizure is serious and is a signal that assets should be fully protected from that moment forward.

The IRS keeps a record of when each warning is made to protect itself from charges by taxpayers that they didn't know the IRS was going to make the seizure and to assure itself that IRM procedure is being followed.

Taxpayers who comply with the instructions in IRS notices to respond promptly, or who comply with the demands of collection employees, will avoid having their property seized. If you can't pay your taxes in full, attempt to arrange an installment agreement, an extension of time to borrow the money, or a determination that you cannot pay at the current time.

If you fail to cooperate, or fail to work out a compromise or extension agreement with the IRS, the IRS will begin the actual seizure process.

Serving a Notice of Levy to seize a paycheck or bank account is simple: The form is completed and either mailed or served personally on the bank or employer. Even though most levy notices are served on banks and employers, they can actually be served on any person or business entity that owes you any amount of money for any reason.

The seizure of tangible personal property or real property is more involved. The Revenue Officer must first determine that there is need to seize.

The determination to seize usually depends on the activity or inactivity of the taxpayer. At some point in the collection process, contact is usually made with the taxpayer and a plan of action is specified. The Revenue Officer's decision will usually be to grant a sixty-day extension to borrow the money, negotiate an installment agreement, demand full payment, or declare the tax uncollectible due to financial hardship.

If you do not earnestly attempt to pay off your taxes, either by trying to borrow the money or by making payments on a periodic basis, and if you do not cooperate, by not returning phone calls, or not keeping appointments, you are issuing an invitation to the IRS to exercise their powers to seize whatever they can get their hands on. Revenue Officers are under pressure to close cases promptly, and they do not waste much time with an uncooperative taxpayer.

Because making a seizure takes time and effort, most Revenue Officers prefer not to if there is a quicker way to close the case. But there are Revenue Officers who enjoy

exercising legal muscle. Also, some IRS managers push their officers to make seizures for the sole purpose of enhancing their statistical profile. So the need to close a case promptly, the need to take enforcement action as retribution against an uncooperative taxpayer, and the need to accumulate seizure statistics may combine to make a seizure unavoidable.

Once the officer has determined there is a need to seize, he must ascertain what property is available for seizing and compute how much equity you have in the property. If the taxes are owed from individual income taxes (taxes owed from Form 1040 or 1040A), the most likely targets for a seizure are your automobile or house. If the taxes are owed by an employer from his or her employees' withholding taxes, the most likely targets are cash register receipts and furniture or equipment located in the public portions of the business.

Your equity in property is computed by subtracting the amount owed on the property from its fair market value. For example, if you still owe $5,000 on an automobile with a resale value of $8,000, you have equity of $3,000 in the automobile. If you have a $50,000 mortgage on a house worth $80,000, you have equity of $30,000 in the house.

If the equity is substantial and far in excess of the tax liability, the Revenue Officer may decide not to seize it. There is no specific rule, but the equity should be sufficient to pay the taxes and all expenses without having too much equity lost in the sale.

IRS policy prohibits Revenue Officers from seizing property when the equity in the property is insufficient "to yield net proceeds from sale to apply to the unpaid tax liabilities". Furthermore, any officer who seizes such property must release it immediately. If it is determined that there is sufficient equity in the seized property to pay for the expenses of sale, but the net proceeds from the sale will be small in comparison to the tax liability, the officer and his group manager must decide if pursuing the seizure and sale is warranted.

Before seizure can be made, the

Revenue Officer must obtain the concurrence of his group manager. If the property to be seized is your personal residence, the seizure must also be approved above the group manager's level. If the property is a going business, the officer must exercise every reasonable effort to collect the tax on a voluntary basis.

The purpose of seizing property is to sell it for cash and apply the cash to the tax liability. Once seizure has been made, the Revenue Officer is required to demand full payment of the tax liability and reimbursement of expenses and costs before the property can be returned to you. Do not be misled by this demand for full payment, however, Code Section 6343(a) authorizes the release of a seizure if the action will facilitate collection of the tax, and the regulations pursuant to Section 6343(a) specify the conditions under which a release can be made. But IRS policy requires that when seized property is released prior to sale for less than immediate full payment, that "subsequent full payment must be provided for."

Many taxpayers believe that once their property has been seized they can't get it back. Many Revenue Officers do not make it a practice to inform taxpayers that this is not so. Even the IRS seizure forms given to the taxpayer are unclear on this point.

How to Get IRS Seizures Released

There are several effective methods that can be used to obtain a release of seized property. These methods work on any type of seizure from bank accounts and paychecks to homes and automobiles. Of course, the IRS will release a seizure any time the taxes are paid in full.

Code Section 6343(a) authorizes the release of a seizure upon all or part of the seized property if it is determined that the action will facilitate collection of the tax liability. The regulations to this section specify the conditions that must exist before the levy can be released, and IRM policy requires that subsequent full payment must be provided for.

Releasing a Notice of Levy is not a procedure that is followed strictly. Many IRS employees who have the authority to serve levies have the authority to release them at their own discretion. Since releasing a levy does not normally require supervisory approval, collection employees can issue a release without being accountable for their actions.

But don't be mistaken. Collection employees usually release levies only when convinced there is a good reason to do so. One reason is when you can't pay your taxes and the levy would appear to be creating a financial hardship. However, neither the Tax Code, the regulations, nor IRM policy provide for a release of levy when it is clear that the levy is creating a financial hardship for you and/or your family. But levies are released for this reason every day, because most collection employees are compassionate and realize that if you can't pay the taxes and pay necessary living expenses at the same time, the case is "uncollectible." And if the case is uncollectible prior to levy, it is uncollectible subsequent to levy.

However, it is one thing to be able to obtain a release of a Notice of Levy served on your paycheck or bank account due to financial hardship, and quite another to obtain a release of a personal or real property seizure for the same reason. A seizure of personal or real property involves the participation of too many participants for the Revenue Officer to exercise discretion that is not specifically allowed. Levies or seizures of any type of property may be released for full payment or for the following conditions provided subsequent full payment is provided for. Also, just because a levy or seizure has been released, it does not avoid the possibility of future levy action.

According to IRS regulations, a levy or a seizure may be released under the following conditions:

- *Escrow Arrangement.* Although rarely used, this benefits businesses that have assets or inventory under seizure. The escrow arrangement ensures payment either when large tax liabilities are involved or when there are conditions peculiar to a particular case. Property is placed in escrow with a reliable and disinterested third party who assumes control of it for the purposes of protecting the property and securing payment of the liability. The escrow arrangement can be particularly effective in a situation in which the IRS has a particular asset under seizure, such as an entire business, and the taxpayer needs to have property released in order to raise money to pay the taxes.

- *Bond.* You may obtain a release of levy by delivering an acceptable bond to the IRS, conditioned upon payment of the delinquent taxes. IRS regulations specify what constitutes an acceptable bond.

- *Payment of amount of U.S. interest in the property.* This does not apply to seizures of monetary assets such as bank accounts and paychecks, but it is important when the IRS has seized a tangible non-monetary asset like a car or a home. IRM policy defines the value of the government's interest in the property to mean either fair market value or forced sale value. Obviously it is to your benefit to select the forced sale value figure since it is always lower than the fair market value. The government's true interest in seized property is the forced sale value because the forced sale value is a better reflection of the property's distressed condition. This provision is one that can be of the most value to you. There is no need to allow the IRS to sell your property at a forced sale liquidation price solely because you do not have the money to pay the taxes in full at the time of sale.

- *Release where value of the interest of the IRS is insufficient to meet the expenses of sale.* Although the Tax Code allows the IRS to seize property or rights to property to collect taxes, it does not prevent the IRS from seizing property in which the taxpayer has small equity. For many years, officers have seized property in which the taxpayer had no equity. This was solely a practice of harassment. Officers know from experience that 80 to 90 percent of the tangible property seizures never go to sale, because the taxpayer somehow comes up with the money to pay the tax delinquency and obtain a property release or redemption. Occasionally the IRS has to sell the seized property when the taxpayer simply does not have the money to pay the taxes and does not know how the property could be released without paying the taxes in full. Sometimes, seized property with little or nominal equity was sold to strangers solely for payment of expenses. Since this had no effect upon reducing the taxpayer's tax liability, the seizure and sale were unjustified.

When it is clear that the sale of the property will not even pay IRS expenses of seizure and storage, the IRS can save face by releasing your seized property. If the officer has done his job properly, this situation would never arise in the first place, because officers are now prohibited from making seizures of property in which you have no equity. IRM 5341.21(5) requires the officer to immediately release seized property if your equity is insufficient to yield net proceeds from the sale to apply to the unpaid tax.

But officers are still acting within IRS policies and procedures if they seize property with nominal equity and sell the property at a price just more than sufficient to pay the expenses.

The only saving grace of the IRS is that they are a plodding bureaucracy. Though they financially grind down people who owe them, they do so relatively slowly. Usually, you have two to six months after the tax due date before the IRS will actually start seizing assets, assuming you have ignored them

Many taxpayers attempt to beat the IRS by transferring the titles to assets before the IRS files liens or seizes.

Transferring property, if properly and lawfully done, can be as effective in protecting yourself from the IRS as from other creditors. But you have to be very careful. Timing is a crucial element in determining whether or not the action is legal. In some situations a transfer of assets to another person or to another form of ownership could be an "earmark of fraud" if it was intended to hinder, delay, or defraud creditors. A transfer of assets may be considered a "fraudulent conveyance" if the intention was to place the property beyond the reach of creditors to the detriment of their rights. Some states have enacted statutes making it a criminal offense to participate in a fraudulent conveyance as it was discussed in Chapter 2.

This can be confusing, and so before discussing it any further, a distinction needs to be made between three separate actions. The first is the actual change in legal ownership of assets (a change in title). The second is the removal of assets from one locality to another, an action called "concealment." The third is the specific act of hiding and not reporting income to the IRS, a clearly illegal act called "evasion." This discussion pertains solely to a change in ownership rights, and not to any illegal act of evasion through under-reporting of income or taxes, or concealment where you lie to the IRS about the location of assets to which it has seizure rights.

Section 7206(4) of the Tax Code makes it a felony to remove, deposit, or conceal any property upon which a levy has been authorized, with the intention of evading or defeating the assessment or collection of any tax. An example of such a violation would

completely. So if you really cannot pay and you can't borrow, (it is better to owe almost *anyone* but the IRS) you can at least delay collection until you can dig up the money.

Transferring Assets to Beat The IRS

occur if your employer purposely pays you an advance to preclude the IRS from levying upon your accrued salary. One taxpayer ploy is to transfer their bank account. Revenue Officers are frequently frustrated by this action, and there is not much they can do about it. As long as the taxpayer actually had the bank account on the particular date that he told the IRS he had the account, perjury was not committed. (Remember that all the payment and financial agreement forms and the "Collection Information Statement," Form 433-A, are signed under penalty of perjury.) Taxpayers frequently change bank accounts, and doing so is not considered concealment unless the taxpayer puts his money in an account under a fictitious name, or commingles it with the account of another person or business entity. It is not uncommon for an IRS levy sent to a bank to be returned because the "account is closed." When this occurs they try to find either the taxpayer's current banks or something else to seize.

Revenue Officers sometimes have difficulty finding a taxpayer's car. The taxpayer may sell his car legitimately and then borrow or lease one for use. At other times, the vehicle is just not to be found. This is another collection frustration because officers do not have the authority to force a taxpayer to produce property for seizure.

Since possession is a major factor in protecting the government's interest in property, Revenue Officers are required to seize property if there is any indication that other creditors will also attempt to repossess or attach the property or that the taxpayer may dispose of the property to the detriment of the government.

The law does not prevent a person from selling his assets even if there are outstanding liens on the property. Under most state laws the liens would remain with the property after a transfer or sale has been made. The IRS would not even question the sale of property encumbered with tax liens unless it appeared that the sale was for "less than good and valuable consideration."

Revenue Officers who discover fraudulent conveyances are usually powerless to do anything about them. Each procedure must be run through the bureaucratic maze for approval. Court suits sometimes take years and cost the government thousands of dollars in staff time. Administrative assessments take months. Unless it is absolutely necessary to pursue these remedies, collection will take some other direction.

How to Compromise Your IRS Liability

It is not well known that you can oftentimes work out payment plans with the IRS. There is hardly any way of escaping owed taxes — not failure to pay, not bankruptcy, not death (owed taxes are taken out of your estate first). You can, however, prevent the IRS from seizing assets by filing a Chapter 13. Under a Chapter 13, the IRS, like other creditors, must avoid further collection efforts over the 3 year payment period.

But even the IRS cannot collect more than you own or what you can reasonably afford to pay. So to resolve tax debts the IRS commonly enters into "offers and compromises" by which it may accept a small fraction of what is owed, and even then may accept payments over a term of years.

How does the IRS decide what compromise amount it will accept? According to the IRS it first considers the liquidation value of your assets. But remember the IRS is first to be paid (after mortgage holders). Therefore, you may decide to sell or honestly transfer the property well before a tax lien is placed. If you do have assets, obtain the lowest possible legitimate appraisal for purposes of establishing a "low value" for your property.

The IRS also considers your future earning ability and the net surplus available after reasonable living expenses. Again, the IRS is not concerned with your general creditors because the IRS has priority. However, if you're about to land a high paying job it may be best to work out your compromise agreement with the IRS before the new paychecks begin.

Very few people understand the "secret" rules by which the IRS collects its debts. But now you have at your fingertips an actual copy of the official IRS manual used to guide tax collectors. This valuable information is contained at the end of this chapter.

Official "offer and compromise" forms are available at any office of the Internal Revenue Service and can be easily completed.

IRS TAX COLLECTION GUIDELINES

COLLECTION ACTIVITY

5223

Analysis of Taxpayer's Financial Condition

(1)   The analysis of the taxpayer's financial condition provides the interviewer with a basis to make one or more of the following decisions:

   (a)   require payment from available assets;

   (b)   secure a short-term agreement or a longer installment agreement;

   (c)   report the account currently not collectible;

   (d)   recommend or initiate enforcement action (this would also be based on the results of the interview);

   (e)   file a Notice of Federal Tax Lien; and/or

   (f)   explain the offer in compromise provisions of the Code to the taxpayer.

(2)   In all steps that follow, information on the financial statement will be compared with other financial information provided by the taxpayer, particularly the copy of the taxpayer's latest Form 1040. If there are significant discrepancies, they should be discussed with the taxpayer. In the event further documentation is needed, it will be the taxpayer's responsibility to provide it. Discrepancies and their resolution will be noted in the case file history.

(3)   Analyze assets to determine ways of liquidating the account:

   (a)   if the taxpayer has cash equal to the tax liability, demand immediate payment;

   (b)   otherwise, review other assets which may be pledged or readily converted to cash (such as stocks and bonds, loan value of life insurance policies, etc.);

   (c)   if necessary, review any unencumbered assets, equity in encumbered assets, interests in estates and trusts, lines of credit (including available credit on bank charge cards), etc., from which money may be secured to make payment. In addition, consider the taxpayer's ability to make an unsecured loan. If the taxpayer belongs to a credit union, the taxpayer will be asked to borrow from that source. Upon identification of potential sources of loans, establish a date that the taxpayer is expected to make payments; and

   (d)   if there appears to be no borrowing ability, attempt to get the taxpayer to defer payment of other debts in order to pay the tax first.

(4)   When analysis of the taxpayer's assets has given no obvious solution for liquidating the liability, the income and expenses should be analyzed.

(a)   When deciding what is an allowable expense item, the employee may allow:

1.   expenses which are necessary for the taxpayer's production of income (for example, dues for a trade union or professional organization; child care payments which allow a taxpayer to work);

2.   expenses which provide for the health and welfare of the taxpayer and family. The expense must be reasonable for the size of the family and the geographic location, as well as any unique individual circumstances. An expense will not be allowed if it serves to provide an elevated standard of living, as opposed to basic necessities. Also, an expense will not be allowed if the taxpayer has a proven record of not making the payment. Expenses allowable under this category are:

a.   rent or mortgage for place of residence;

b.   food;

c.   clothing;

d.   necessary transportation expense (auto insurance, car payment, bus fare, etc.);

e.   home maintenance expense (utilities, home-owner insurance, home-owner dues, etc.);

f.   medical expenses; health insurance;

g.   current tax payments (including federal, state and local);

h.   life insurance, but not if it is excessive to the point of being construed as an investment;

i.   alimony, child support or other court-ordered payment.

3.   Minimum payments on secured or legally perfected debts (car payments, judgments, etc.) will normally be allowed. However, if the encumbered asset represents an item which would not be considered a necessary living expense (e.g., a boat, recreational vehicle, etc.), the taxpayer should be advised that the debt payment will not be included as an allowable expense.

4.   Payments on unsecured debts (credit cards, personal loans, etc.) may not be allowed if omitting them would permit the taxpayer to pay in full within 90 days. However, if the taxpayer cannot fully pay within that time, minimum payments may be allowed if failure to make them would

ultimately impair the taxpayer's ability to pay the tax. The taxpayer should be advised that since all necessary living expenses have been allowed, no additional charge debts should be incurred. Generally, payments to friends or relatives will not be allowed. Dates for final payments on loans or installment purchases, as well as final payments on revolving credit arrangements after allowing minimum required payments, will be noted so the additional funds will be applied to the liability when they become available. If permitting the taxpayer to pay unsecured debts results in inability to pay or in only having a small amount left for payment of the tax, the taxpayer should be advised that a portion of the money available for payment of debts will be used for payment of the taxes and that arrangements must be made with other creditors accordingly.

(b) As a general rule, expenses not specified in (a) above will be disallowed. However, an otherwise disallowable expense may be included if the employee believes an exception should be made based on the circumstances of the individual case. For instance, if the taxpayer advises that an educational expense or church contribution is a necessity, the individual circumstances must be considered. If an exception is made, document the case history to explain the basis for the exception.

(c) The taxpayer will be required to verify and support any expense which appears excessive based on the income and circumstances of that taxpayer. However, proof of payment does not automatically make an item allowable. The criteria in (4)(a) apply.

(d) In some cases, expense items or payments will not be due in even monthly increments. For instance, personal property tax may be due once a year. Unless the taxpayer substantiates that money is being set aside on a monthly basis, the expense will be allowed in total in the month due and the payment agreement adjusted accordingly for that month. Expense items with varying monthly payments should be averaged over a twelve-month period unless the variation will be excessive. In such instances, exclude the irregular months from the average. For example, if a utility bill will be excessive during the three winter months, average the other nine months.

(e) In arriving at available net income, analyze the taxpayer's deductions to ensure that they are reasonable and allowable. The only automatically allowable deductions from gross pay or income are federal, state and local taxes (including FICA or other mandatory retirement program).

1. Other deductions from gross pay or income will be treated and listed as expenses, but only to the extent they meet the criteria in (4)(a) above.

2. To avoid affording the taxpayer a double deduction for one expense, ensure that such amounts remain in the total net pay figure and are also entered on the expense side of the income and expense analysis.

3. If the exemptions on the W-4 are going to be decreased, make the appropriate adjustments in the net income figures.

(f) To reach an average monthly take-home pay for taxpayers paid on a weekly basis, multiply the weekly pay times 52 weeks divided by 12 months (or multiply amount times 4.3 weeks). If the taxpayer is paid biweekly, multiply pay times 26 weeks divided by 12 months (or multiply amount times $2\,1/6$). If the taxpayer is paid semimonthly, multiply pay times 2.

(g) The amount to be paid monthly on an installment agreement payment will be at least the difference between the taxpayer's net income and allowable expenses. If the taxpayer will not consent to the proposed installment agreement, he/she should be advised that enforced collection action may be taken. The taxpayer should also be advised that an appeal of the matter may be made to the immediate manager.

(5) When an analysis of the taxpayer's financial condition shows that liquidation of assets and payments from present and future income will not result in full payment, consider the collection potential of an offer in compromise.

5225

Verification of Taxpayer's Financial Condition

(1) In some cases it will be necessary or desirable to obtain additional information about the taxpayer's financial condition. The extent of the investigation will depend upon the circumstances in each case.

(2) If items appear to be over- or understated, or out of the ordinary, the taxpayer should be asked to explain and substantiate if necessary. The explanation will be documented in the case history. If the explanation is unsatisfactory or cannot be substantiated, the amount should be revised appropriate to the documentation available.

5231.1

General Installment Agreement Guidelines

(1) When taxpayers state inability to pay the full amount of their taxes, installment agreements are to be considered.

(2) Future compliance with the tax laws will be addressed and any returns and/or tax due within the period of the agreement must be filed and paid timely.

(3) Levy source information, including complete addresses and ZIP codes, will be secured.

(4) Equal monthly installment payments should be requested. Payment amounts may be increased or decreased as necessary.

(5) Once the determination is made that the taxpayer has the capability to make a regular installment payment, that agreement will be monitored through routine provisions unless the payment amount is less than $10 (in which case the account should be reported currently not collectible). The major benefits of this approach are issuance of reminder and default notices (if the account is system-monitored) and enforcement action if the agreement is not kept.

(6) The taxpayer should be allowed to select the payment due date(s). But if there is no preference, the date when the taxpayer would generally be in the best financial position to make the payment(s) should be chosen.

(7) If the interviewer and the taxpayer cannot agree on the amount of installments, the taxpayer should be advised that an appeal may be made to the immediate manager.

(8) An installment agreement which lasts more than two years must be reviewed at the mid-point of the agreement, but in no event less than every two years.

Levy and Sale

5311

Introduction and General Concepts

(1)   Under the Internal Revenue Code, levy is defined as the power to collect taxes by distraint or seizure of the taxpayer's assets. Through levy, we can attach property in the possession of third parties or the taxpayer. Generally, a notice of levy is used to attach funds due the taxpayer from third parties. Levy on property in possession of the taxpayer is accomplished by seizure and public sale of the property. There is no statutory requirement as to the sequence to be followed in levying, but it is generally less burdensome and time consuming to levy on funds in possession of third parties.

(2)   Levy authority is far reaching. It permits a continuous attachment of the non-exempt portion of the wage or salary payments due the taxpayer, and the seizure and sale of all the taxpayer's assets except certain property that is specifically exempt by law. Prior to levying on any property belonging to a taxpayer, the Service must notify the taxpayer in writing of the Service's intention to levy. The statute does not require a judgment or other court order before levy action is taken. The Supreme Court decision in the matter of *G.M. Leasing Corporation v. United States,* 429 U.S. 338 (1977), held that an entry without a warrant and search of private areas of both residential and business premises for the purpose of seizing and inventorying property pursuant to Internal Revenue Code section 6331 is in violation of the Fourth Amendment. Prior to seizure of property on private premises, a consent to enter for the purpose of seizing or writ of entry from the local courts must be secured.

(3)   Procedures are designed (except in jeopardy cases) to give taxpayers a reasonable chance to settle their tax liabilities voluntarily before the more drastic enforcement actions are started. At least one final notice must be issued before service of a notice of levy.

(4)   Under the self-assessment system, a taxpayer is entitled to a reasonable opportunity to voluntarily comply with the revenue laws. This concept should also be followed in connection with levy action. This does not mean that there should be a reluctance to levy if the circumstances justify that action. However, before levy or seizure is taken on an account, the taxpayer must be informed, except in jeopardy situations, that levy

or seizure will be the next action taken and given a reasonable opportunity to pay voluntarily. Once the taxpayer has been advised and neglects to make satisfactory arrangements, levy action should be taken expeditiously, but not less than 10 days after notice.

(5) Notification prior to levy must be given in accordance with (2) above. It should be specific that levy action will be the next action taken. In the event the service center has not sent the taxpayer the 4th notice which includes notice of intention to levy at least 10 days before the levy, the revenue officer must provide the notice to the taxpayer as indicated in (2) above.

(6) A notice of levy should be served only when there is evidence or reasonable expectation that the third party has property or rights to property of the taxpayer. This concept is of particular significance, since processing of notices of levy is time consuming and often becomes a sensitive matter if it appears the levy action was merely a "fishing expedition."

5312

Statutory Authority to Levy

(1) IRC 6331 provides that if any person liable to pay any tax neglects or refuses to pay the tax within 10 days after notice and demand, the tax may be collected by levy upon any property or rights to property belonging to the taxpayer or on which there is a lien.

(2) IRC 6331 also provides that if the Secretary determines that the collection of tax is in jeopardy, immediate notice and demand for payment may be made and, upon the taxpayer's failure to pay the tax, collection may be made by levy without regard to the 10-day period. However, if a sale is required, a public notice of sale may not be issued within the 10-day period unless IRC 6336 (relating to sale of perishable goods) is applicable.

(3) Under the IRC, the term "property" includes all property or rights to property, whether real or personal, tangible or intangible. The term "tax" includes any interest, additional amount, addition to tax, or assessable penalty, together with any cost that may accrue.

(4) Generally, property subject to a Federal tax lien which has been sold or otherwise transferred by the taxpayer, may be levied upon in the hands of the transferee or any subsequent transferee. However, there are exceptions for securities, motor vehicles and certain retail and casual sales.

(5) Levy may be made on any person in possession of, or obligated with respect to, property or rights to property subject to levy. These include, but are not necessarily limited to, receivables, bank accounts, evidences of debt, securities and accrued salaries, wages, commissions, and other compensation.

(6) The IRC does not require that property be seized in any particular sequence. Therefore, property may be levied upon regardless of whether it is real or personal, tangible or intangible, and regardless of which type of property is levied upon first.

(7) Whenever the proceeds from the levy on any property or rights to property are not sufficient to satisfy the tax liability, additional levies may be made upon the same property, or source of income or any other property or rights to property subject to levy, until the account is fully paid. However, further levies should be timed to avoid hardship to the taxpayer or his/her family.

5314.1

Property Exempt From Levy

(1) IRC 6334 enumerates the categories of property exempt from levy as follows.

   (a) *Wearing apparel and school books necessary for the taxpayer or for members of his family*—No specific value limitation is placed on these items since the intent is to prevent seizing the ordinary clothing of the taxpayer or members of the family. Expensive items of wearing apparel, such as furs, are luxuries and are not exempt from levy.

   (b) *Fuel, provisions and personal effects*—This exemption is applicable only in the case of the head of a family and applies only to so much of the fuel, provisions, furniture, and personal effects of the household and of arms for personal use, livestock, and poultry as does not exceed $1,500 in value.

   (c) *Books and tools of a trade, business or profession*—This exemption is for so many of the books and tools necessary for the trade, business, or profession of the taxpayer as do not exceed in the aggregate $1,000 in value.

(d) *Unemployment benefits*—This applies to any amount payable to an individual for unemployment (including any portion payable to dependents) under an unemployment compensation law of the United States, any state, the District of Columbia or the Commonwealth of Puerto Rico.

(e) *Undelivered mail*—Addressed mail which has not been delivered to the addressee.

(f) *Certain annuity and pension payments.*

(g) *Workmen's compensation*—Any amount payable to an individual as workmen's compensation (including any portion payable to dependents) under a workmen's compensation law of the United States, any state, the District of Columbia, or the Commonwealth of Puerto Rico.

(h) *Judgment for support of minor children*—If the taxpayer is required by judgment of a court of competent jurisdiction, entered prior to the date of levy, to contribute to the support of his/her minor children, so much of his/her salary, wages, or other income as is necessary to comply with such judgment.

(i) *Minimum Exemption from Levy on Wages, Salary and Other Income*—IRC 6334(a)(9) limits the effect of levy on wages, salary and other income, by an amount of $75 per week for the taxpayer and an additional $25 a week for the spouse and each dependent claimed by the taxpayer. Income not paid or received on a weekly basis will, for the purpose of computing exemptions, be apportioned as if received on a weekly basis.

(2) In addition, Public Law 89-538 exempts deposits to the special Treasury fund made by servicemen and servicewomen (including officers) and Public Health Service employees on permanent duty assignment outside the United States or its possessions.

(3) Except for the exemptions in (1) and (2) above, no other property or rights to property are exempt from levy. No provision of state law can exempt property or rights to property from levy for the collection of federal taxes. The fact that property is exempt from execution under state personal or homestead exemption laws does not exempt the property from federal levy.

(4) The revenue officer seizing property of the type described in (1)(a), (b), and (c) above should appraise and set aside to the owner the amount of property to be exempted.

538(10)

Records of Attorneys, Physicians, and Accountants

(1) Records maintained by attorneys, physicians, and accountants concerning professional services performed for clients are usually of little intrinsic value and possess minimum sale value. Questions of confidential or privileged information contained in these records may cause complications if the records are seized. Additionally, the case files of the professional person frequently either are, or contain, property of the client, and therefore to this extent are not subject to seizure. Accordingly, it is not believed desirable to seize case files or records for payment of the taxpayer's tax liabilities.

(2) When office facilities or office equipment of attorneys, physicians, or public accountants are seized for payment of taxes, case files and related files in seized office facilities or office equipment of such persons will not be personally examined by the revenue officer even though information concerning accounts receivable may be contained in the files. When storage facilities (filing cabinets, etc.) are seized, the taxpayer should be requested to remove all case files promptly.

583(11)

Safe Deposit Boxes

538(11).1

General

(1) The procedures outlined below should be followed in an attempt to secure the opening of a taxpayer's safe deposit box in instances in which the taxpayer's consent to or cooperation in opening the box cannot be obtained.

(2) Ordinarily two keys are used to open a safe deposit box: a master key held by the bank or trust company which owns the box and an individual key in the possession of the person who rents the box.

(3) Irrespective of the possession of the necessary equipment to do so, it is not to be expected that a bank or trust company will open a safe deposit box without the consent of the lessee of the box unless protected by a court order. Under these

circumstances the government must prevent the taxpayer from having access to the box, or obtain a court order directing that the box be opened, by force if necessary.

(4)   At the time that a safety deposit is secured, Publication 787, Seal for Securing Safety Deposit Boxes, will be signed by the revenue officer and affixed over the locks for security while the box remains under seizure. When the box is eventually opened, all residue from the seal should be removed by the revenue officer, or the bank official in the revenue officer's presence, with isopropyl alcohol or a similar solvent. To avoid damage to the safety deposit box, no sharp implement or abrasive substance should be used. The seal will dissolve when saturated with alcohol and rubbed with a cloth.

583(11).2

Preventing Access to Safe Deposit Box

(1)   A notice of lien should be filed prior to seizure since assets other than cash may be in the safe deposit box.

(2)   A notice of levy, Form 668-A, with a copy of the notice of lien attached, should be served on an officer of the bank or trust company and request made for surrender of the contents of the box.

(3)   The official may advise that the institution does not have the necessary key to open the safe deposit box or that the institution does not have the authority to open it. He/she may also suggest that the lessee's (taxpayer's) consent be secured, or that a court order be obtained to open the box.

(4)   Under these circumstances, the revenue officer should not insist that the box be opened and no attempt should be made to have the box opened by force. The box should be sealed by affixing a seizure notice, Publication 787, Seal for Securing Safety Deposit Boxes. It should be placed over the locks in such a manner so that the box cannot be opened without removing, tearing or destroying the affixed seal. The bank or trust company should then be advised not to permit the box to be opened except in the presence of a revenue officer.

(5)   Usually, taxpayers who have been reluctant to cooperate will eventually find it necessary to open their boxes, and will only be able to do so in the presence of a

revenue officer. At that time, the revenue officer, with Form 668-B in his/her possession, will be in a position to seize any property in the box.

(6) When the rental period of the safe deposit box expires and is not renewed, a bank or trust company usually has the right and power to open the box. The revenue officer should attempt to ascertain the true situation in any given case, and if the right and power exists, should try to take advantage of this opportunity to seize the contents of the box.

538(11).3

Obtaining Court Order To Open

(1) Occasionally, the procedure outlined in IRM 538(11).2 will not be satisfactory and immediate action may be desirable or necessary. For instance, the statute of limitations may be about to expire, the taxpayer may have disappeared or be in concealment, or the taxpayer or bank officials may refuse cooperation and deny access to a safe deposit box.

(2) Under these circumstances a Summons should be prepared and served on the taxpayer-boxholder in an attempt to secure information as to the contents of the box and to gain access. If this action does not accomplish the desired results, a writ of entry should be sought or a suit requested to open the safe deposit box.

Currently Not Collectible Accounts

5610

Determination of Currently Not Collectible Taxes

5611

General

(1) A Collection employee may determine that the accounts are currently not collectible.

(2) Reporting an account currently not collectible does not abate the assessment. It only stops current efforts to collect it. Collection can start again any time before the statutory period for collection expires.

5632

Unable-To-Pay Cases—Hardship

5632.1

General

(1) If collection of the liability would prevent the taxpayer from meeting necessary living expenses, it may be reported currently not collectible under a hardship closing code. Sometimes accounts should be reported currently not collectible even though the Collection Information Statement (CIS) shows assets or sources of income subject to levy.

  (a) [The Manual] provides guidelines for analyzing the taxpayer's financial condition.
  (b) Since each taxpayer's circumstances are unique, other factors such as age and health must be considered as appropriate.
  (c) Document and verify the taxpayer's financial condition.
  (d) Consider the collection potential of an offer in compromise.

(2) Consider an installment agreement before reporting an account currently not collectible as hardship.

Offers in Compromise

5712

Grounds for Compromise

5712.1

General Guidelines

The compromise of a tax liability can only rest upon doubt as to liability, doubt as to collectibility, or doubt as to both liability and collectibility. IRC 7122 does not confer authority to compromise tax, interest, or penalty where the liability is clear and there is no doubt as to the ability of the Government to collect. To compromise there must be room for mutual concessions involving either or both doubt as to liability or doubt as to ability to pay. This rules out, as ground for compromise, equity or public policy considerations peculiar to a particular case, individual hardships, and similar matters which do not have a direct bearing on liability or ability to pay.

5713.2

Advising Taxpayers of Offer Provisions

(1) When criminal proceedings are not contemplated and an analysis of taxpayer's assets, liabilities, income and expenses shows that a liability cannot realistically be paid in full in the foreseeable future, the collection potential of an offer in compromise should be considered. While it is difficult to outline the exact circumstances when an offer would be the appropriate collection tool, the existence of any of the following should govern offer consideration.

    (a) Liquidation of assets and payments from present and future income will not result in full payment of tax liability.

    (b) A non-liable spouse has property which he/she may be interested in utilizing to secure a compromise of spouse's tax debt.

    (c) The taxpayer has an interest in assets against which collection action cannot be taken. For example, the taxpayer who owes a separate liability, has an interest in property held in "tenancy by the entirety" which cannot be reached or subjected to the Notice of Federal Tax Lien because of the provisions of state law. Under the compromise procedures, the taxpayer's interest is included in the total assets available in arriving at an acceptable offer in compromise.

(d) The taxpayer has relatives or friends who may be willing to lend or give the taxpayer funds for the sole purpose of reaching a compromise with the Service.

5721

General

The offer in compromise is the taxpayer's written proposal to the Government and, if accepted, is an agreement enforceable by either party under the law of contracts. Therefore, it must be definite in its terms and conditions, since it directly affects the satisfaction of the tax liability.

5723.1

Prescribed Form

A taxpayer seeking to compromise a tax liability based on doubt as to collectibility must submit Form 433, Statement of Financial Condition and Other Information. This form includes questions geared to develop a full and complete description of the taxpayer's financial situation.

5723.3

Refusal To Submit Financial Statement

If a taxpayer professing inability to pay refuses to submit the required Form 433, the offer will be immediately rejected since the Service cannot determine whether the amount offered is also the maximum amount collectible.

5725.1

Liability of Husband and Wife

(1) Under IRC 6013(d)(3), the liability for income tax on a joint return by husband and wife is expressly made "joint and several." Either or both of the spouses are liable for the entire amount of the tax shown on a joint return. When the liability of both parties is sought to be compromised, the offer should be submitted in the names of

and signed by both spouses in order to make the waiver and other provisions of the offer form effective against both parties.

(2) An "innocent spouse" may be relieved of liability in certain cases under IRC 6013(e) and IRC 6653(b). In the event that one of the jointly liable taxpayers claims to be an "innocent spouse," the question should be referred to the district Examination function for determination.

(a) Should the offer be acceptable, the report should not be prepared until after the district Examination function has made its determination. Since a favorable decision for the party claiming "innocent spouse" will change the amount of the liability sought to be compromised, any recommendation for acceptance must reflect the redetermined liability.

5740

Investigation of Offers

5741.1

General

(1) Once an offer in compromise is received in Special Procedures function, a determination whether the offer merits further consideration must be made. SPf should use all information contained in the offer file and may consult with the revenue officer assigned the TDAs [tax deficiency assessments] to obtain additional financial information or verify existing information.

(2) Summary rejection in SPf can be made on the grounds that the offer is frivolous, was filed merely to delay collection, or where there is no basis for compromise. A desk review of the offer can result in this determination. Although not all-inclusive, the following list provides guidelines on the criteria for summary rejection most often encountered:

(a) Taxpayer has equity in assets subject to the Federal tax lien clearly in excess of the total liability sought to be compromised,

(b) The total liability is extremely large and the taxpayer has offered only a minimum sum well below his/her equity and earning potential (e.g., offering $100 to compromise a $50,000 tax liability). Although the taxpayer could be persuaded to raise the offer, the fact that this initial amount offered was so low indicates bad faith and the desire to delay collection,

(c) The taxpayer is not current in his/her filing or payment requirements for periods not included in the offer,

(d) The taxpayer refuses to submit a complete financial statement (Form 433),

(e) Acceptance of the offer would adversely affect the image of the government,

(f) Taxpayer has submitted a subsequent offer which is not significantly different from a previously rejected offer and the taxpayer's financial condition has not changed,

(g) In cases involving doubt as to liability for the 100-percent penalty, the liability is clearly established and the taxpayer has offered no new evidence to cast doubt on its validity.

5741.2

Public Policy

(1) An accepted offer, like any contract, is an agreement between two parties resulting from a "meeting of the minds." It is incumbent upon each party to negotiate the best terms possible. Normally, the offer and subsequent negotiations are of a private nature. However, when accepting an offer, the Service is in a unique position since it represents the government's interest in the negotiations and the accepted offer becomes part of public record. Therefore, public policy dictates that an offer can be rejected if public knowledge of the agreement is detrimental to the government's interest. The offer may be rejected even though it can be shown conclusively that the amounts offered are greater than could reasonably be collected in any other manner. Because the Government would be in the position of foregoing revenue, the circumstances in which public policy considerations could be used to reject the offer must be construed very strictly. The following may be used as a guideline for instances where public policy issues are most often encountered:

(a) Taxpayer's notoriety is such that acceptance of an offer will hamper future Service collection and/or compliance efforts. However, simply because the taxpayer is famous or well-known is not a basis in and of itself for rejecting the offer on public policy grounds.

(b) There is a possibility of establishing a precedent which might lead to numerous offers being submitted on liabilities incurred as a result of occupational drives to enforce tax compliance.

(c)   Taxpayer has been recently convicted of tax related crimes. Again, the notoriety of the individual should be considered when making a public policy determination. The publicity surrounding the case, taxpayer's compliance since the case was concluded, or the taxpayer's position in the community should all be considered prior to rejecting an otherwise acceptable offer.

(d)   Situations where it is suspected that the financial benefits of criminal activity are concealed or the criminal activity is continuing would normally preclude acceptance of the offer for public policy reasons. Criminal Investigation function should be contacted to coordinate the Government's action in these cases.

Bankruptcy and Wage Earner Plans

5

Do you know you can take advantage of an important federal law to keep all of your assets while ridding yourself of excess debt? This law is known as Chapter 13 of the Bankruptcy Act, or a "Wage Earner's Plan."

Unfortunately, despite the increase in Chapter 13 filings, many people don't know very much about Chapter 13, the federal debt repayment plan. Indeed, when some first hear about it, they think it must be a part of some book. In a sense they're right.

The whole idea of Chapter 13 is really pretty simple: it permits an individual under court supervision and protection to develop and fulfill a plan to pay his or her debts in whole or in part over a three year period. Or, put in even simpler terms, Chapter 13 means learning to live within a budget, while debts beyond your ability to repay are forgiven.

Filing a Chapter 13 repayment plan is much like taking out a debt consolidation loan. You wipe out all your obligations in exchange for a weekly or monthly payment to an officer of the court called a trustee. Chapter 13, however, is preferable to consolidation loans for five reasons:

Chapter 13 is a part of a very long book known as the bankruptcy laws of the United States. But don't let the fact that it is part of the bankruptcy laws mislead you. For many consumer debtors, *Chapter 13 is a way of avoiding straight bankruptcy,* a means of developing a sense of pride and self-satisfaction in meeting one's obligations, and a highly effective way to prevent creditors from levying on assets.

How Chapter 13 Protects You

1. You pay no interest or finance charges on most debts;

2. You determine the amount of your periodic payments;

3. You decide how much of your debts you are able to repay and cancel those debts you cannot pay;

4. You retain your assets;

5. You are protected from all creditor harassment once you file.

To qualify for this important alternative to straight bankruptcy, you must have a regular income, hence the popular name,

"Wage Earner's Plan." Instead of losing or being forced to sell your property, however, you set up an installment payment program through the court. The payment plan lasts three years and can be extended for two more. You must also set up and must follow a strict budget similar to what a credit counselor would set up for you. You are not allowed to take on any new debt during the pay-back period. The court has the option of waiving missed payments if you fail in the plan through no fault of your own such as unemployment. Once you successfully complete the payment plan, the court will discharge those debts not paid in full. If you cannot complete the program successfully, you may go into straight bankruptcy.

The Bankruptcy Code itself contains several Chapters which provide various forms of relief to different classes of debtors. For example, there is complete discharge in Bankruptcy under Chapter 7 of the Code, while Chapter 13 is a Court supervised debt repayment plan. Then there is a Chapter 11 which is a business reorganization and Chapter 12 which is for the family farmer.

Our focus will be on Chapter 13 of the Bankruptcy Code.

You (the debtor) must have resided in the Bankruptcy District where you plan to file the Petition, the greater part of six months (3 months and 1 day). For example, if the debtor has recently moved into the Bankruptcy District where he or she now resides. then he or she must await the expiration of the period deemed to be the greatest part of six months. In other words, it does not matter where the debts are located, it is residence of the debtor that determines where the action should be filed. Therefore, if the debtor has not resided in the District where he or she is presently residing for the greater part of six months, the action must be commenced in that District where residence was formerly established. This may, of course, mean that it will be necessary to travel some distance to attend the hearing.

It is possible to file the petition by mail and request that the Court temporarily transfer the hearing to the local Bankruptcy Court. This request is not, however, always approved.

Here is an overview of how Chapter 13 works. In Chapter 13, petitions similar to those filed in straight bankruptcy are used where your assets and liabilities are disclosed. A meeting or meetings with creditors and a referee will be held, and you will present your proposed plan for repayment. You need the approval of your secured creditors and a majority of your unsecured creditors for the plan to be approved. The court must then approve your plan. If approved, the court will appoint a trustee who will act much like a credit counselor in overseeing your installment payment program. Obtaining approval is usually not difficult because creditors know that they will receive more through a Chapter 13 plan than if you filed for Chapter 7, and your assets were liquidated to satisfy creditor claims.

To actually "file" a Chapter 13 debt repayment plan, you must complete and file with the Bankruptcy Court the forms found in this chapter, or similar forms found in legal stationery stores. Review them now, but don't be intimidated. All the documents really amount to is a budget showing your monthly income, ordinary living expenses and the amount left over to apply to your debts.

Filling out and filing these forms (check current filing fees) immediately stops all creditor harassment, collection efforts and foreclosure or tax seizure proceedings. Once you file you also stop wage attachments as well as any automatic deductions from your paycheck for debt repayments. From this point forward all payments to your creditors will be made through this court appointed "trustee" following the terms of your repayment plan.

About one month after you file, you must meet with the trustee. The trustee will ask questions about your plan, your debts and your property. The trustee will want to make certain that you were reasonable and responsible when you designed your budget and that your plan therefore has a good chance of success. After meeting with the trustee, you will also have a brief meeting with a bankruptcy judge. If the judge finds that your plan complies with the law, the judge will "confirm" the plan and it will immediately take effect.

Plans typically call for the payment of all, or almost all, of your debts over the three year payment period. During that time, you will pay the trustee a specified amount each month and the trustee will repay your past bills and deal directly with your creditors. You can either send the trustee the regular payment provided in your plan or have it deducted from your paycheck. When you live up to your promise and make all payments under the three year plan, you will return to court for a "discharge" hearing. Because you have kept your promise, the judge will formally forgive any remaining balance due on all debts covered by your plan, except taxes and family support obligations which must be fully paid.

How To Calculate Your Wage Earner's Plan

Since you keep all of your property if you file a Chapter 13 repayment plan, don't worry about losing your home or other assets. But look carefully at your property for another reason: the type and amount of property you own establishes the minimum amount that you will be required to pay under your Chapter 13 plan. The first thing to understand is that both state and federal laws contain lists of "exempt property" — property debtors can keep safe from their creditors even if they were to file for straight bankruptcy. While state laws vary, most exempt items such as the family home, work tools, clothes and household furnishings. These lists of exempt property have a special meaning for debtors who file Chapter 13 plans. The amount of your non-exempt property (that is, property which is not on either the state or federal exempt list) places a bottom limit on the amount of debts you must repay under your Chapter 13 plan. You must make payments that equal or exceed the value of your non-exempt property. A listing of the federal exemptions can be found at the end of this chapter.

This means that to calculate the minimum total payment you must make under your Chapter 13 repayment plan, you must first decide which of your belongings is exempt. From the fair value of your assets, you may deduct assets "exempt" from creditor attachment.

The federal law and each state has its own list of exemptions. In about a third of the states you will have a choice between the two separate exemption systems — one state and the other federal. You can choose either one, but you can't choose some of one and some of the other. It is up to you to compare your state exemption system with the federal exemption system and decide which will be the most advantageous in your situation.

However, in about two-thirds of the states you do not have a choice. You must use the state exemption system even if less favorable. You can easily find out what the exemptions are in your state by contacting bankruptcy legal guides available at any law library.

As of this writing, the federal exemptions list includes: up to $7,500 interest in property that is the home of the debtor, $1,200 interest in a car, household items where any one item does not exceed $200 in value, $500 in jewelry, $750 worth of books and tools of trade, your rights to alimony, support and maintenance payments (unemployment, veterans, disability), benefits from life insurance, pensions, annuities, Social Security, $4,000 in life insurance cash value. Some states exemptions are quite meager compared to the federal exemptions.

But before you file, you may want to consider these tips:

1. If you are due a tax refund, the trustee will claim it for the creditors. You can however, write to the tax agency and ask them to retain the funds toward future taxes. You may also want to wait

for the refund check before filing.

2.   If you expect to receive an inheritance within six months after you file for bankruptcy, talk to your lawyer. Unless you are careful, the inheritance can be claimed to satisfy your debts.

3.   Any property transfers that you may have made up to one year prior to filing in which you did not receive at least fair market value for the exchange can be cancelled by the court, with the property reclaimed and resold to satisfy creditor claims. Consult your lawyer if this situation seems like a possibility. Also, if you make a payment to a credi-

tor within ninety days prior to filing, this may be deemed a preference and recovered from the creditor. The bankruptcy laws attempt to treat all creditors evenly and on a pro-rata basis so the court may recover that money from the creditor and distribute it evenly to the rest of your creditors.

4.   Once you have identified your exempt assets, consider selling some of your non-exempt assets for cash and use this money to purchase exempt assets which are fully protected under the bankruptcy proceeding.

Are All Your Debts Dischargeable?

Before filing be certain sufficient amounts of your debts are dischargeable so Chapter 13 offers a helpful solution. Not all debts are wiped out through Chapter 13. Frequently people rush to file without realizing that their particular debts *will not* be discharged and that their debts were only reduced by a few thousand dollars through the Chapter 13. Debts that cannot be discharged include: 1) alimony, child support and maintenance; 2) taxes due less than three years, or taxes filed fraudulently or not at all; 3) debts to the extent of the value of any property that is pledged as collateral against said debt; 4) debts where you obtain consideration through the use of theft, fraud or embezzlement; 5) debts where the lender extended the credit on the basis of a false financial statement or application; 6) debts incurred, such as with a credit card, just before filing if the debtor had no intent to pay; 7) liabilities incurred because of willful or malicious injuries to a person or his property; 8) certain student loans — if less than five years old and repayment won't cause undue hardship; 9) penalties and fines due a government; and 10) any debts not listed on your filing petition.

Bankruptcy will however wipe (discharge) all unsecured debts as long as there is no proof of fraud, false pretenses or

false representations involved. Examples of dischargeable debts are as follows:

1. Attorney fees

2. Civil suit judgments

3. Collection agency accounts

4. Credit card charges

5. Dishonored checks (unless occasioned by fraud)

6. Federally insured school tuition loans (under certain conditions)

7. Medical bills (all types)

8. Open account charges

9. Past due rent

10. Repossession deficiency balances

11. Revolving charge accounts

12. School tuition loans (non-insured)

13. Unsecured signature loans

14. Utility bills (past due)

15. Veterans assistance loans

Divide your debts into two categories: dischargeable and non-dischargeable. Don't forget to include as non-dischargeable those debts you elect to reaffirm or pay back such as to family, a friend (or for another personal or business reason). If the total amount that would be cancelled through bankruptcy is small or a small portion of your total debt, it probably won't be worth the expense, trouble, and negative effects on your credit to file for bankruptcy. A professional advisor may help you find more appropriate alternatives.

Under the 1979 amendments to the Bankruptcy laws, a debtor was given the right to redeem exempt personal property that was subject to a creditor's otherwise valid lien.

What this means is that if the debtor has household furnishings (or other exempt personal property) that is subject to a creditor's lien, he or she can file a motion to redeem such property at its market or appraised value.

Usually the only objection the creditor will make is that the value of the property is in dispute. This of course means that the debtor must be prepared to prove the validity of his or her stated value of the property.

The clear advantage here is that almost all personal property (for example, household furnishings, automobiles, bicycles, sewing machines, etc.) depreciates rapidly in value with age. Therefore, it is not uncommon for such personal property to be valued as low as ten to twenty percent (or lower) of its purchase price.

There is however a requirement that when the motion to redeem the property is granted by the Court, the debtor must pay to the creditor in full (one payment), the amount found to be the market value of the property.

There are four types of liens against your property which can be set aside under either a straight bankruptcy (Chapter 7) or Wage Earner's Plan (Chapter 13).

Unsecured Realty Liens

This type of avoidable lien came into recognition as a result of several Bankruptcy Court Rulings which found substance in the fact that if a realty lien is not secured by the value of the real property, then it is an unsecured lien subject to a lien avoidance action.

Redeeming Mortgaged Property

An example of what this means is that if the debtor owns a house (or mobile home, condominium, townhouse, etc.) with a market value of $30,000 which has a first mortgage of $30,000 and a second mortgage of $5,000, then the second mortgage is not secured since the total of both mortgages exceeds the market value of the property with the second being inferior to the first.

When the motion to avoid lien is filed with the Court, there will be a hearing in which proof of the market value of the property will have to be decided by the Court from the evidence submitted by both sides.

Judicial Liens

This type of lien arises as a result of a Court judgment. In other words, if the debtor was the defendant in a lawsuit seeking a money judgment, and the Court subsequently entered a judgment against the defendant (debtor) for a certain sum of money, then this judgment, when properly recorded, becomes a lien against whatever real property is owned by the Defendant.

This lien can be avoided if it attaches to the homesteaded real or personal property of the debtor. Keep in mind that the property must be exempt property under either state law or the Federal Bankruptcy Code, whichever is applicable.

Purchase Money Lien

This type of lien is created under an installment contract that allows the debtor to purchase property with monthly payments. Some of the most common examples of a Purchase Money Lien is, for example:

(1)   Automobile purchase contracts,

(2)   Furniture installment contracts,

(3)   Department store time pay contracts,

(4)   Encyclopedia installment contracts, etc.

The distinguishing characteristic of a purchase money contract is that actual (legal) title to the property does not pass to the buyer until the final payment is made to the creditor. This, of course, is clearly stated in one of the clauses normally referred to as the "fine print" in the contract.

In other words, the lien cannot represent the balance due from the initial installment purchase price of the property.

Non-Purchase Money Lien

This broad definition of liens includes virtually all types of consensual liens where money is loaned together with a lien being lodged against some specific property of the debtor.

If a personal loan is secured by all (or most) of the debtor's household furnishings or goods, and the loan does not represent any part of the purchase price of such furnishings or goods, then the lien created under this type of loan is avoidable under this section.

Some bankruptcy courts have decided that this action applies to loans secured by automobiles when the loan does not represent any part of the purchase price of the vehicle.

Answers to Important Questions About Chapter 13

A Wage Earner's Plan need not be overly complex but like most legal matters, Chapter 13 repayment plans do become more complicated, especially when you fill in the general picture with more detail. None of the rules are difficult, but some rules are more difficult to understand the first time you read them. So let's answer some of the more common questions people ask about Chapter 13 Wage Earner Plans.

Q. What's the difference between straight bankruptcy (Chapter 7) and a Chapter 13 repayment plan?

A. Straight bankruptcy is a debtor's most powerful weapon. It is a way to make most debts completely disappear with no need to repay them. Straight bankruptcy is often preferred if someone realistically cannot expect to pay a significant portion of his or her debts and has few or no assets to preserve. A Wage Earner's Plan is primarily for the individual who has a home or other assets he wishes to retain while cancelling debts in excess of his equity in the property.

Q. Can I file a Chapter 13 plan if I once filed for straight bankruptcy?

A. Yes. You can file for straight bankruptcy only once every six years, but you can file a Chapter 13 plan anytime, regardless of prior bankruptcy or prior Chapter 13 proceedings or when they occurred.

Q. How much does a Chapter 13 proceeding cost?

A. You must pay a $90 fee when you file your repayment plan with the court. The court will also charge a small fee to administer your plan, but this charge will be deducted automatically from your regular payments. The cost will certainly be a lot less that the interest, finance charges and late charges you paid creditors before filing your plan.

Q. How long do I have to repay my debts under a Chapter 13 plan?

A. Most repayment plans take three years, although a court can accept or compel a five year plan.

Q. Is there a limit on the amount of debts under a Chapter 13 plan?

A. Yes. You must owe less than $100,000 in unsecured debts and $300,000 in secured debts. If you owe more, you cannot use Chapter 13.

Q. Do I have to pay 100% of my debts under a Chapter 13 plan?

A. No. It works like this. Deduct your ordinary living expenses from your monthly income. Whatever is left will be paid to your creditors over the term of your repayment plan. If you successfully complete your plan, all of your debts — except taxes and family support obligations and other non-dischargeable debts — will disappear, even though you might not have paid your creditors in full. Bear in mind, though, that if you can't pay all, or almost all, of your debts over the three year term of your plan, Chapter 13 may not be the best solution to your financial problems.

Q. What happens if my creditors won't agree to my repayment plan?

A. Filing a Chapter 13 plan is your decision alone. If you are willing to make an honest effort, and your plan is approved by the bankruptcy court, your creditors can't adversely affect the success of the plan.

Q. Will I lose my property if I don't pay all of my debts in full under the plan?

A. Probably not. Filing a Chapter 13 plan is one way to keep all of your property, even though you are unable to pay your debts in full. There is one exception to this general rule. If a creditor sold you some property or loaned you the money to buy it and you made a written promise that, if you did not pay, the creditor could take the property back (such as through a mortgage), you must keep that promise and pay the creditor either whatever the property is worth or the amount you owe, whichever is less. If you don't pay, you must give the property back or surrender it for foreclosure.

Q. What happens to debts co-signed by friends or relatives?

A. If a friend or relative co-signed your loan, they will have to pay whatever portion of the debts you do not pay under your Chapter 13 plan. You are not legally required to reimburse your friend or relative if this occurs; therefore, whether you do or not is a matter between you and your friend or relative.

Q. Should my spouse and I both file repayment plans?

A. If you are married, it is usually best for you and your spouse to file a Chapter 13 plan together if each of you has incurred debts. If only one spouse files, you run the risk of the other spouse's creditors getting a judgement and directing the sheriff to seize property. This may upset your financial affairs and prevent you from successfully completing your repayment plan. If only one spouse has debts, however, only that indebted spouse should file.

Q. Do I have to be working in order to file a Chapter 13 repayment plan?

A. No—but you must have some stable and regular source of income such as wages, earnings from self-employment or investments, pensions, social security or public benefits to qualify as a "wage earner" since the court will look for a source of income to insure your repayment.

Q. Will my employer know about my Chapter 13 or my repayment plan?

A. Your employer need not know. You can choose to make regular payments directly to the trustee yourself rather than have payments withheld from your paycheck. Even if you choose to have payments made by your employer, it's unlikely your employer will care if you file a Chapter 13 proceeding. In fact, both private employers and governmental agencies are forbidden to fire you merely because you file a Chapter 13 plan. Nevertheless, there are some kinds of jobs that may be jeopardized by filing a Chapter 13 plan, particularly work in which the employee must be bonded, such as a bank teller. If you have any concerns about the impact of a Chapter 13 on your job, be sure to consult with your employer before you file.

Q. What will a Chapter 13 repayment proceeding do to my credit rating?

A. Credit reporting agencies are allowed to keep a notation of your Chapter 13 proceedings on file for 10 years. They list the total amount of your debts and specify how much you repaid under your repayment plan. It is then up to individual creditors to decide what to do with that information. Most creditors already know of your difficulties with debts and, against this background, a Chapter 13 filing is likely to be viewed as a favorable step forward as it shows you are willing to make an honest effort to meet your commitments. Re-establishing a perfect credit rating won't happen overnight, of course, but when you find you must proceed slowly when gaining new credit it is probably a blessing in disguise.

Q. Do I need a lawyer in order to file a Chapter 13 repayment plan?

A. No. Filing a Chapter 13 plan is often easier than preparing your income tax return. If you can accomplish that, you can probably handle your repayment plan yourself.

Q. How much will a lawyer charge me to handle a Chapter 13?

A. A typical fee is between $500-$750 ($1,000 for a husband and wife), however, many attorneys advertise fees as low as $200 plus filing fees so it may pay to discuss fees with several attorneys.

How To File Your Own Wage Earner's Plan

At the end of this chapter you will find a complete set of Chapter 13 forms (note: forms and local court rules are subject to change). Here are detailed instructions on how to complete these documents and where and how to file:

1) Use a typewriter to neatly complete each form exactly as shown. If you can't type, photocopy the forms and fill in a set by hand. Then have someone type the information on the original copy of each form. You must use a legible type on the typewriter.

Most of the instructions are on the sample forms. Where longer explanations are needed, you will be directed to detailed instructions that will follow the form.

Don't worry if you run out of room on any of the forms. Just take a blank sheet of white paper, the same size as the forms, label it "additional page to (title of form)" and type in the additional data.

2) Filling in these forms is not difficult. You already have all the information you need. But it can be a little tedious, so take your time. You don't have to get all the work done at once.

A few courts and trustees prefer that you use their particular version of Form #3 (Chapter 13 plan) as well as prepare a separate analysis or summary of your plan on their prescribed forms. You may want to check with your local bankruptcy court.

In addition, some courts may require that the debtor submit a special form or order to be signed by the judge at the confirmation hearing. Again, be sure to check with the bankruptcy clerk about any special local requirements.

3) Make four xerox copies of each form. You must file the original and 3 copies of Forms #1-5 with the clerk of the bankruptcy court to start your Chapter 13 proceeding. The fourth xerox copy of each form is for you to keep in your own file.

Take the five sets of Forms #1-5 (the original and four copies) together with the filing fee, $90 in cash (or certified check), to the clerk of the bankruptcy court in your judicial district.

"File" your Chapter 13 plan by handing

the 5 sets of those forms and $90 in cash to the clerk. The clerk will give you a receipt and return to you one full set of forms marked "filed" with the date in the upper right hand corner and stamped with the number of your case on each form. Keep these in your file.

It is also possible to file by mail. Instead of sending cash, enclose a $90 money order or certified check payable to the U.S. Bankruptcy Clerk. It is preferable to file in person so that you will have the opportunity to clear up any questions you or the court may have about filing papers or how things are handled in court. Bankruptcy clerks can be very helpful with these matters, but their ability to assist you with any other legal questions you may have is quite limited as they are not allowed to give legal advice.

4) After filing, contact the court appointed trustee who will have responsibility for your case. Try to meet with the trustee as soon as possible so you can properly proceed with the plan. The court clerk can give you the name of the trustee.

5) If your wages are being attached or money is being taken out of your paycheck for your credit union, notify your employer right away of your Chapter 13 filing so that he or she can stop taking those deductions from your paycheck. Do this in writing unless you have a good personal relationship with your employer. Also, mail a copy of your Chapter 13 petition to the sheriff and your credit union if they are involved so that they will stop asking for the automatic deductions. Similarly, notify the mortgagee or lender threatening repossession or foreclosure of your home or personal property.

6) Don't worry about your other creditors. The court will notify them of your Chapter 13 filing using the list of labels (3 copies of matrix) that you supplied with your bankruptcy petition. You don't have to do it. Upon notification, they must immediately stop all harassment, bill collection efforts, wage garnishments, lawsuits, foreclosures and repossessions. If any of your creditors should contact you in the week or so between your filing and their notification by the court, simply tell them of your Chapter 13 filing and give them the number which the clerk stamped on the first page of your Chapter 13 forms. If they don't believe you, tell them to call the bankruptcy court. If your creditors persist, you may wind up having grounds to sue them or having the bankruptcy court hold them in contempt.

PROPERTY EXEMPTIONS
UNDER THE FEDERAL
BANKRUPTCY ACT

TYPE OF PROPERTY EXEMPTED	STATUTES CREATING THE EXEMPTIONS	MAXIMUM AMOUNT EXEMPTED
Real or Personal Property used as a residence (includes Mobile Home) or a Burial Plot.	11 U.S.C. §522(d)(1)	$7,500.00
One Motor Vehicle.	11 U.S.C. §522(d)(2)	1,200.00
All items of household furnishings, goods and appliances.	11 U.S.C. §522(d)(3) (per item)* (See No. 1 below)	200.00
All items of wearing apparel.	11 U.S.C. §522(d)(3) (per item)* (See No. 1 below)	200.00
All items of: Books, Animals, Crops or Musical Instruments	11 U.S.C. §522(d)(3) (per item)* (See No. 1 below)	200.00
Jewelry (total value of all pieces)	11 U.S.C. §522(d)(4)	500.00
Professional Books, Tools of Trade and Implements	11 U.S.C. §522(d)(6)	750.00
Professionally prescribed Health Aids.	11 U.S.C. §522(d)(9)	any amount
Social Security Benefits, Unemployment Compensation, Public Assistance, Veterans Benefits, Alimony, Support, Separate Maintenance, Payments under a Stock Plan, Profit Sharing Plan, Annuity or other plan for the reason of illness, disability, death, age or length of service.	11 U.S.C. §522(d)(10)	any amount
An Award under the Crime Victims Reparation Law	11 U.S.C. §522(11)(A)	any amount
Life Insurance payments when debtor is the dependent of the insured.	11 U.S.C. §522(d)(11)(C)	any amount
A payment for the wrongful death of an individual of whom debtor was a dependent.	11 U.S.C. §522(d)(11)(B)	any amount
A payment for loss of future earnings of a debtor or an individual upon who debtor is dependent	11 U.S.C. §522(d)(11)(E)	any amount
Debtor's interest in any other property not particularly itemized in this Schedule	11 U.S.C. §522(d)(5)* (See No. 2 below)	400.00
A portion of the amounts not used under Section 522(d)(1) above to exempt Real or Personal property used as a residence or burial plot may be used under this statute to exempt any other property whether or not such property has been previously claimed under a previous statute.[2]	11 U.S.C. §522(d)(5)* (See No. 2 below)	3,750.00

NOTE: Under the 1984 amendments to the Bankruptcy Code, husband and wife debtors cannot claim separate exemptions under both the Federal Exemption Laws and the State Statutes. In other words, they must both claim their exemptions under the same set of laws. This is, of course, assuming that the Federal Exemption Laws apply in the State where you plan to file your action

---

[1]The maximum amount that can be exempted under this Section 522(d)(3) is an aggregate total of $4,000.00.

[2]Under this statute, any amount left over (not exceeding $3,750.00) after applying the allowed exemption to a residence or burial plot can be used to exempt other property whether previously exempted or not scheduled. For example, Boats, Airplanes, Income tax refunds, exempt wages, etc.

Exempt Property Under Other Federal Laws

There are various Federal Laws, other than the Federal Bankruptcy Laws, that provide for the exemption of certain property. These exemptions, as scheduled below, can be used in a Bankruptcy Action if there does not exist an applicable State or Federal Bankruptcy Exemption Statute which specifically exempts the possessed property. An example of this application is: (1) Income received under the Social Security Act, (2) Railroad Retirement Act, (3) Federal Civil Service Retirement Act, etc.

Property Exempted	Federal Statute
The earnings of a debtor subject to process is limited to a maximum of 25% of disposable earnings.	15 U.S.C. § 1673
Railroad Employees Retirement Benefits under the Railroad Retirement Act.	45 U.S.C. § 228(L)

Property Exempted	Federal Statute
All lands acquired by Federal Homestead Laws.	43 U.S.C. § 175
All Veterans Administration proceeds, including Veterans pensions, U.S. Life Insurance Benefits, pensions and disability allowances.	38 U.S.C. § 3101
Any and all benefits under the Social Security Act.	42 U.S.C. § 407
Retirement benefits under the Federal Civil Service or Employees Retirement Fund.	5 U.S.C. § 8346

CHAPTER 13 PETITION
AND SCHEDULES

UNITED STATES BANKRUPTCY COURT FOR THE   DISTRICT OF _____

Date Petition Filed _____
Case Number _____
Bankruptcy Judge _____

In re

Debtor*

}

CHAPTER 13
VOLUNTARY PETITION
& EXHIBIT "B"

Soc. Sec. No. _____ Debtor's Employer's Tax Id. No. _____

(If this form is used for joint petitioners wherever the word "petitioner" or words referring to petitioner are used they shall be read as if in the plural.)

1. Petitioner's mailing address, including county, is

2. Petitioner has   ☐   resided within this district for the preceding 180 days.
              ☐   had his(*her*) domicile within this district for the preceding 180 days.
              ☐   had his(*her*) principal place of business within this district for the preceding 180 days.
              ☐   had his(*her*) principal assets within this district for the preceding 180 days.
              ☐   resided or been domiciled or had his(*her*) principal place of business within this district for a longer portion of the preceding 180 days than in any other district.

3. Petitioner is qualified to file this petition and is entitled to the benefits of title 11, United States Code as a voluntary debtor.

4.   ☐   A copy of petitioner's proposed plan, dated _____ 19___ is attached.
      ☐   Petitioner intends to file a plan pursuant to chapter 13 of title 11, United States Code.

5.   A declaration in the form of Exhibit "B" is attached to and made a part of this petition.[1]

Wherefore, petitioner prays for relief in accordance with chapter 13 of title 11, United States Code.

Petitioner(s) signs if not represented by attorney

Signed: _____
         Attorney for Petitioner

_____
               Petitioner

Address: _____

_____

_____
               Petitioner

DECLARATION

INDIVIDUAL: I, _____ the petitioner named in the foregoing petition, declare under penalty of perjury under the laws of the United States that the foregoing is true and correct.

JOINT INDIVIDUALS: We, _____ and _____ the petitioners named in the foregoing petition, declare under penalty of perjury under the laws of the United States that the foregoing is true and correct.

Executed on _____ 19___   Signature: _____
                                                   Petitioner

_____
                                                   Petitioner

EXHIBIT "B"

I, _____ the attorney for the petitioner named in the foregoing petition, declare that I have informed the petitioner that he or she may proceed under chapter 7 or 13 of title 11, United State Code, and have explained the relief available under each such chapter.

Executed on _____   Signature of Attorney for Petitioner

*Set forth here all names including tradenames used by Debtor within last 6 years.

[1]This paragraph applies if petitioner is an individual whose debts are primarily consumer debts and petitioner is represented by an attorney, otherwise delete.

In re

Debtor*

} **CHAPTER 13 STATEMENT**

Soc. Sec. No.   Debtor's Employer's Tax Id. No.

(If this form is used by joint debtors wherever the word "debtor" or words referring to debtor are used they shall be read as if in the plural.)

    Each question shall be answered or the failure to answer explained. If the answer is "none" or "not applicable" so state. If additional space is needed for the answer to any question, a separate sheet, properly identified and made a part hereof, should be used and attached.

    The term, "original petition," used in the following questions, shall mean the original petition filed under § 301 of the Code or, if the chapter 13 case was converted from another chapter of the Code, shall mean the petition by or against you which originated the first case.

    This form must be completed in full whether a single or a joint petition is filed. When information is requested for "each" or "either spouse filing a petition" it should be supplied for both when a joint petition is filed.

1. **Name and residence** *(b)* Where does debtor, if single, or each spouse filing a petition now reside?   (3) Telephone number
    (a) Give full name   (1) Mailing address, (2) City or town, state and zip code   including area code

    Husband [or, *if single*, Debtor]

    Wife

    (c) What does debtor, if single, or each spouse filing a petition consider his or her residence, if different from that listed in (b) above?

        Husband [*or* Debtor]

        Wife

2. **Occupation and income** *(a)* Give present occupation of debtor, if single, or each spouse filing a petition. (If more than one, list all for debtors or each spouse filing a petition.)

        Husband [*or* Debtor]

        Wife

    (b) What is the name, address, and telephone number of present employer (or employers) of debtor, if single, or each spouse filing a petition? (Include also any identifying badge or card number with employer.)

        Husband [*or* Debtor]

        Wife

    (c) How long has debtor, if single, or each spouse filing a petition been employed by present employer?

        Husband [or Debtor]   Wife

    (d) If debtor or either spouse filing a petition has not been employed by present employer for a period of 1 year, state the name of prior employer(s) and nature of employment during that period.

        Husband [*or* Debtor]

        Wife

    (e) Has debtor or either spouse filing a petition operated a business, in partnership or otherwise, during the past 3 years? (If so, give the particulars, including names, dates, and places.)

        Husband [*or* Debtor]

        Wife

(f) Answer the following questions for debtor, if single, or each spouse whether single or joint petition is filed unless spouses are separated and a single petition is filed:

(1) What are your gross wages, salary or commissions per pay period?

	Husband [or Debtor]	Wife
(a) Weekly	$ _____	$ _____
(b) Semi-monthly	$ _____	$ _____
(c) Monthly	$ _____	$ _____
(d) Other (specify)	$ _____	$ _____

(2) What are your payroll deductions per pay period for:

	Husband [or Debtor]	Wife
(a) Payroll taxes (including social security)	$ _____	$ _____
(b) Insurance	$ _____	$ _____
(c) Credit union	$ _____	$ _____
(d) Union dues	$ _____	$ _____
(e) Other (specify)	$ _____	$ _____
(f) _____	$ _____	$ _____
(g) _____	$ _____	$ _____

(3) What is your take-home pay per period? Husband [or Debtor]$_____ Wife $ _____

(4) What was the amount of your gross income for the last calendar year? Husband [or Debtor] $_____ Wife $ _____

(5) Is your employment subject to seasonal or other change? Husband [or Debtor] $_____ Wife $ _____

(6) Has either of you made any wage assignments or allotments? (If so, indicate which spouse's wages assigned or allotted, the name and address of the person to whom assigned or allotted, and the amount owing, if any, to such person. If allotment or assignment is to a creditor, the claim should also be listed in Item 11a.)

3. **Dependents** (To be answered by debtor if unmarried, otherwise for each spouse whether single or joint petition is filed unless spouses are separated and a single petition is filed.)

(a) Does either of you pay [or receive] alimony, maintenance or support?   If so, how much per month?
For whose support? (Give name, age, and relationship to you.)

Husband [or Debtor]

Wife

(b) List all other dependents, other than present spouse, not listed in (a) above. (Give name, age, and relationship to you.)

Husband [or Debtor]

Wife

4. **Budget** (*a*) Give your estimated average future monthly income if unmarried, otherwise for each spouse
whether single or joint petition is filed, unless spouses are separated and a single petition is filed.

    (1) Husband's (or Debtor's) monthly take-home pay _____ $ _____

    (2) Wife's monthly take-home pay _____ $ _____

    (3) Other monthly income (specify) _____ $ _____

    (4) _____ $ _____

    (5) _____ $ _____

    (6) _____ $ _____

    (7) _____ Total $ _____

(*b*) Give estimated average future monthly expenses of family (not including debts to be paid under plan), consisting of:

    (1) Rent or home mortgage payment (include lot rental for trailer) _____ $ _____

    (2) Utilities (Electricity $_____ Heat $ _____ Water $_____ Telephone $ _____) $ _____

    (3) Food_____ $ _____

    (4) Clothing _____ $ _____

    (5) Laundry and cleaning_____ $ _____

    (6) Newspapers, periodicals, and books (including school books) _____ $ _____

    (7) Medical and drug expenses_____ $ _____

    (8) Insurance (not deducted from wages): (a) Auto $ _____ (b) Other $ _____ _____ $ _____

    (9) Transportation (not including auto payments to be paid under plan) _____ $ _____

    (10) Recreation _____ $ _____

    (11) Dues, union, professional, social or otherwise (not deducted from wages)_____ $ _____

    (12) Taxes (not deducted from wages) _____ $ _____

    (13) Alimony, maintenance, or support payments _____ $ _____

    (14) Other payments for support of dependents not living at home _____ $ _____

    (15) Other (specify):_____ $ _____

             _____ $ _____

             _____ $ _____

             _____ $ _____

             _____ $ _____

             _____ Total $ _____

(*c*) Excess of estimated future monthly income (last line of Item 4(a) above) over estimated future exp.
(last line of Item 4(b) above) _____ $ _____

(*d*) Total amount to be paid each month under plan _____ $ _____

5. **Payment of attorney**

    (*a*) How much have you agreed to pay or what property have you agreed to transfer to your attorney in
connection with this case? _____ $ _____

    (*b*) How much have you paid or what have you transferred to the attorney? _____ $ _____

6. **Tax refunds*** To what tax refunds (income or other), if any, is either of you, or may either of you be entitled? (Give particulars,
including information as to any refunds payable jointly to you or any other person. All such refunds should also be listed in Item 13(b).)

7. **Financial accounts, certificates of deposit and safe deposit boxes***

   (a) Does either of you currently have any accounts or certificates of deposit or shares in banks, savings and loan, thrift, building and loan and homestead associations, credit unions, brokerage houses, pension funds and the like? (If so, give name and address of each institution, number and nature of account, current balance, and name and address of every other person authorized to make withdrawals from the account. Such accounts should also be listed in Item 13(b).)

   (b) Does either of you currently keep any safe deposit boxes or other depositories? (If so, give name and address of bank or other depository, name and address of every other person who has a right of access thereto, and a brief description of the contents thereof, which should also be listed in Item 13(b).)

8. **Prior Bankruptcy** What proceedings under the Bankruptcy Act or Bankruptcy Code have previously been brought by or against you or either spouse filing a petition? (State the location of the bankruptcy court, the nature and number of each proceeding, the date when it was filed, and whether a discharge was granted or denied, the proceeding was dismissed, or a composition, arrangement, or plan was confirmed.)

9. **Foreclosures, executions, and attachments*** *(a)* Is any of the property of either of you, including real estate, involved in a foreclosure proceeding, in or out of court? (If so, identify the property and the person foreclosing.)

   (b) Has any property or income of either of you been attached, garnished, or seized under any legal or equitable process within the 90 days immediately preceding the filing of the original petition herein? (If so, describe the property seized, or person garnished, and at whose suit.)

10. **Repossessions and returns*** Has any property of either of you been returned to, repossessed, or seized by the seller or by any other party, including a landlord, during the 90 days immediately preceding the filing of the original petition herein? (If so, give particulars, including the name and address of the party taking the property and its description and value.)

11. **Transfers of Property*** *(a)* Has either of you made any gifts, other than ordinary and usual presents to family members and charitable donations, during the year immediately preceding the filing of the original petition herein? (If so, give names and addresses of donees and dates, description and value of gifts.)

(b) Has either of you made any other transfer, absolute or for the purpose of security, or any other disposition, of real or personal property during the year immediately preceding the filing of the original petition herein? (Give a description of the property, the date of the transfer or disposition, to whom transferred or how disposed of, and, if the transferee is a relative or insider, the relationship, the consideration, if any, received therefor, and the disposition of such consideration.)

12. **Debts** (To be answered by debtor, if unmarried, otherwise for each spouse whether single or joint petition is filed.)

(a) *Debts Having Priority.*

(1) Nature of claim	(2) Name of creditor and complete mailing address, including zip code	(3) Specify when claim was incurred and the consideration therefor: when claim is subject to setoff, evidenced by a judgment, negotiable instrument, or other writing	(4) Indicate if claim is contingent, unliquidated, or disputed	(5) M(D) W or J	(6) Amount of claim
1. Wages, salary, and commissions, including vacation, severance and sick leave pay owing to employees not exceeding $2,000 to each, earned within 90 days before filing of petition or cessation of business (if earlier specify date).					$
2. Contributions to employee benefit plans for services rendered within 180 days before filing of petition or cessation of business (if earlier specify date).					
3. Deposits by individuals, not exceeding $900 for each for purchase, lease, or rental of property or services for personal, family, or household use that were not delivered or provided.					
4. Taxes owing (itemize by type of tax and taxing authority) (A) To the United States (B) To any state (C) To any other taxing authority					
				Total	

(b) *Secured Debts.*—List all debts which are or may be secured by real or personal property. (Indicate in sixth column, if debt payable in installments, the amount of each installment, the installment period (Monthly, weekly, or otherwise) and number of installments in arrears, if any. Indicate in the last column whether husband or wife solely liable, or whether you are jointly liable.)

Creditor's name, account number and complete mailing address, Including zip code	Consideration or basis for debt	Amount claimed by creditor	If disputed, amount admitted by debtor	Description of collateral (include year and make of automobile)	Installment amount, period, and number of installments in arrears	Husband or wife solely liable, or jointly liable

Total secured debts $ _____

12. Debts (Continued)

(c) *Unsecured Debts.*—List all other debts, liquidated and unliquidated, including taxes, attorneys' fees and tort claims.

Creditor's name, account number and complete mailing address, including zip code	Consideration or basis for debt	Amount claimed by creditor	If disputed, amount admitted by debtor	Husband or wife solely liable, or jointly liable

(a) Total debts having priority $ _____

(b) Total secured debts $ _____

(c) Total unsecured debts $ _____

Total (a) + (b) + (c) $ _____

13. Codebtors (To be answered by debtor, if unmarried, otherwise for each spouse whether single or joint petition is filed.)

(a) Are any other persons liable, as cosigners, guarantors or in any other manner, on any of the debts of either of you or is either of you so liable on the debts of others? (If so, give particulars, indicating which spouse liable and including names of creditors, nature of debt, names and addresses of codebtors, and their relationship, if any, to you.)

(b) If so, have the codebtors made any payments on the debts? (Give name of each codebtor and amount paid by codebtor.)

(c) Has either of you made any payments on the debts? (If so, specify total amount paid to each creditor, whether paid by husband or wife, and name of codebtor.)

14. **Property and Exemptions** (To be answered by debtor, if unmarried, otherwise for each spouse whether single or joint petition is filed.)

(a) *Real Property.*—List all real property owned by either of you at date of filing of original petition herein. (Indicate in last column whether owned solely by husband of wife, or jointly.)

Description and location of property	Name of any co-owner other than spouse	Present market value (without deduction for mortgage or other security interest)	Amount of mortgage or other security interest on this property	Name of mortgage or other secured creditor	Value claimed exempt. (Specify federal or state statute creating the exemption)	Owned solely by husband or wife, or jointly

(b) Personal Property.—List all other property owned by either of you at date of filing of original petition herein.

Description	Location of property if not at debtor's residence	Name of any co-owner other than spouse	Present market value (without deduction for mortgage or other security interest)	Amount of mortgage or other security interest on this property	Name of mortgage of other secured creditor	Value claimed exempt. (Specify federal or state statute creating the exemption)	Owned solely by husband or wife, or jointly
Auto (give year and make):							
Household goods:							
Personal effects:							
Cash or financial account:							
Other (specify):							

Unsworn Declaration under Penalty of Perjury
(To be signed by both spouses when joint petition is filed.)

I (*We*) _____ and _____ declare under penalty of perjury under the laws of the United States that I (*we*) have read the answers contained in the foregoing statement, consisting of _____ sheets, and that they are true and complete to the best of my (*our*) knowledge, information, and belief.

Executed on _____ 19___   _____   _____
                                     Signature Husband (or Debtor)   Signature (Wife)

Attorney for Debtors & Address _____

_____

UNITED STATES BANKRUPTCY COURT FOR THE   DISTRICT OF _____   Case No.

In re

_____

Debtor, Soc. Sec. No.
[Include here all names used by debtor within last 6 years.]

}

CHAPTER 13
PLAN

(If this form is used by joint debtors wherever the word "debtor" or words referring to debtor are used they shall be read as if in the plural.)

1. The future earnings of the debtor are submitted to the supervision and control of the trustee and the *debtor — debtor's employer* shall pay to the trustee the sum of $ _____ *weekly — bi-weekly — semi-monthly — monthly.*

2. From the payments so received, the trustee shall make disbursements as follows:

    (a) The priority payments required by 11 U.S.C. §507.

    (b) After the above payments, dividends to secured creditors whose claims are duly proved and allowed as follows:

    (c) *Subsequent to — pro rata with* dividends to secured creditors, dividends to unsecured creditors whose claims are duly proved and allowed as follows:

3. The following executory contracts of the debtor are rejected:

       Title to the debtor's property shall revest in the debtor *on confirmation of a plan — upon dismissal of the case after confirmation pursuant to 11 U.S.C. §1329 — upon closing of the case pursuant to 11 U.S.C. §350.*

Dated: _____

_____   _____
      Debtor   *Debtor*

Acceptances may be mailed to _____ _____
                                              Post Office Address

BANKRUPT NAME & ADDRESS	ATTORNEY(S) NAME & ADDRESS	BANKRUPT/DEBTOR NO.
DISTRICT DIRECTOR INTERNAL REVENUE SERVICE DISTRICT OFFICE ADDRESS	START A-Z LIST OF CREDITORS	

DO NOT TYPE IN THIS AREA

If a debt is disclosed to the United States other than one for taxes, type an address for the United States Attorney for the district in which the case is pending and to the department, agent or instrumentality of the United States through which the bankrupt became indebted.

Check with your local district for addresses of state or local government agencies to which addressed label must be prepared.

In re

_____

_____ Debtor*

Soc. Sec. No. _____ Debtor's Employer's Tax Id. No. _____

} SCHEDULE OF
CURRENT INCOME
AND CURRENT
EXPENDITURES

If this form is used by joint debtors wherever the question requires separate answers for Husband (H), Wife (W) or Joint (J) insert the appropriate symbol in column headed H, W or J.

Current Income

A. Give your current monthly income if unmarried, otherwise for each spouse whether single or joint petition is filed, unless spouses are separated and a single petition is filed.

H, W or J

(1) Debtor's monthly take-home pay _____ _____ $_____
(2) Spouse's monthly take-home pay _____ _____ $_____
(3) Regular income available from operation of a business or profession _____ _____ $_____
(4) Do you receive alimony, maintenance or support payments?
      If so, state monthly amount _____ _____ $_____
      State the name, age and relationship to you of persons for whose benefit payments are received

      _____
      _____
      _____

(5) Pension, social security or retirement income _____ _____ $_____

(6) Other monthly income (specify) _____ _____ $_____
      _____ $_____
      _____ $_____
      _____ $_____
      _____ $_____
      _____ Total $_____

Current Expenditures

B. Give current monthly expenditures of family, consisting of: H, W or J

      (1) Rent or home mortgage payment (include lot rental for trailer) _____ _____ $_____
      (2) (Electricity $_____ Heat $_____ Water $_____ Telephone $_____) _____ $_____
      (3) Food _____ _____ $_____
      (4) Clothing _____ _____ $_____
      (5) Laundry and cleaning _____ _____ $_____
      (6) Newspapers, periodicals, and books (including school books)_____ _____ $_____
      (7) Medical and drug expenses _____ _____ $_____
      (8) Insurance (not deducted from wages): (a) Auto $_____ (b) Other $_____ _____ $_____
      (9) Transportation _____ _____ $_____
      (10) Recreation _____ _____ $_____
      (11) Dues, union, professional, social or otherwise (not deducted from wages)_____ _____ $_____
      (12) Taxes (not deducted from wages) _____ _____ $_____
      (13) Alimony, maintenance, or support payments_____ _____ $_____
           State the name, age and relationship to you of persons for whose benefit payments are made

           _____
           _____

      (14) Other payments for support of dependents not living at home _____ _____ $_____
      (15) Expenditures deducted from wages (specify)_____ _____ $_____
           _____ _____ $_____
           _____ _____ $_____
           _____ _____ $_____

      (16) Other (specify) _____ _____ $_____
           _____ _____ $_____
           _____ _____ $_____
           _____ _____ $_____
           _____ $_____
           _____ Total $_____

*Set forth here all names including tradenames used by Debtor within last 6 years.

Homestead and Exemption Protection 6

Surprisingly few people realize there are a number of federal and state laws specifically enacted to protect important assets considered vital to the basic financial integrity and independence of a debtor and his or her family. These laws include homestead laws to protect a family home, and other specific exemptions applicable to insurance, retirement plans and wage income.

Homestead laws may provide you and your family considerable protection from creditor claims levied against the family home.

All but six states provide a homestead exemption designed to safeguard the family residence for the debtor and his or her family. This homestead exemption is one of the most valuable rights debtors enjoy and it is therefore vital to take all the procedural steps necessary to claim the homestead exemption if it is available in the state where your primary residence is located.

1. Who and What is Protected?

The homestead exemption generally applies to real estate owned and *occupied* by the debtor. Primarily, the homestead exemption is available on single-family homes. However, in many states it now extends as well to condominiums, apartments, and in some cases to mobile homes, cabins, or other

Homestead Protection

premises that can be claimed as the principal place of residence.

In most states, the debtor must be the head of the household in order to claim the homestead exemption, and the homestead must be used as the family's primary residence. But once a homestead has been established, the exemption is generally not lost if the debtor temporarily ceases to occupy the residence. In many states the homestead exemption survives death and even divorce. Most states now make the homestead available to single persons.

Typically, only one spouse can make a homestead declaration. If the husband makes the declaration, his wife cannot make one, although she may be a co-owner of the home. Where prohibited, cross-declarations by each spouse for the benefit of the other can backfire with both claims being made invalid.

Tip

> *In states where only one spouse can claim the exemption it should be taken by the spouse with the greatest risk of creditor claims.*

2. Amount of Protection

Unfortunately, homestead laws do not necessarily provide complete protection from creditors. The value, size, and type of property that is eligible for homestead protection varies greatly from jurisdiction to jurisdiction. Most homestead statutes limit the exemption by size, value or both.

Texas, for instance, has perhaps the most liberal homestead statute in the nation: a homestead exemption of 200 rural acres without regard to value, and of $10,000 in value at the time of acquisition of urban property without regard to subsequent improvements. Under these liberal provisions, a $10,000 vacant lot bought in an urban area with improvements of $100,000 would be completely exempt. Similarly, a $500,000 house built on rural property would be completely exempt. In other states, the amount of the exemption is not related to the amount of acreage, but only to the dollar value. Massachusetts, for example, limits the homestead to $100,000. In contrast, Florida has no limitation and even a stately $1 million home would be completely insulated from creditors.

Tip

> *If you live in a state with a relatively small homestead exemption leaving significant equity in your home exposed, then it is best to consider other forms of protection.*

3. Debts Against Which the Homestead is Protected

Exemption laws vary with respect to when a debtor must establish a homestead in relation to when the debt asserted against it arose. Most states allow homestead protection regardless of when the homestead was acquired or declared. In these jurisdictions the debtor may claim exemption merely by asserting it after the sheriff levies on the land or before the property is sold. However, a number of states provide that the homestead is not exempt from debts incurred before it was acquired. In these states it is wise to claim homestead immediately upon taking title.

Homestead may not be effective against certain types of debt. In Florida, for example, there remains uncertainty whether their homestead exemption is effective against IRS tax claims although it is a complete bar to other claims.

Tip

> *Always check with local counsel to determine whether the homestead laws in your state protect you against claims of specific concern.*

Obviously, homestead has no effect on liens voluntarily granted such as mortgages or deeds of trust.

4. Claiming the Homestead Exemption

The judgment debtor or claimant is commonly required to assert the homestead exemption. In many states, the debtor must record a homestead declaration with the official real estate records. Other states provide for an automatic homestead exemption upon occupancy by the homeowner as a principal residence.

Conflicts between judgment lien laws and homestead exemptions often create complex problems. Most states provide that a judgment lien does not attach to homestead property. Thus a purchaser of the homestead property acquires it free of the judgment creditors' claims, even if the purchaser claims no homestead exemption in the purchased property. Conversely, in some states the judgment lien usually does attach to the property, to the extent that the property exceeds the size or value of the allowed homestead exemption.

Tip

> *Inquire whether your home automatically has homestead protection or whether specific steps must be taken to protect your rights.*

5. Problems of Homestead

Although a homestead declaration is

relatively simple to make, it may not be popular in your jurisdiction, or suitable for your purposes for a number of reasons:

1. The most common problem is that the homestead exemption may be too small to provide meaningful protection.

2. You may have exposure to debts that pre-date the homestead or are not protected by homestead, thus leaving your home exposed.

3. A homestead declaration can create title problems for the owners of a property subject to homestead. For example, in many states if the husband died after declaring homestead, his wife probably could not sell or refinance the home without having a guardian ad litem appointed to approve the sale or refinancing as being in the best interests of her minor children. Moreover,

a homestead declaration may need to be released to place a mortgage on the home. While these legal technicalities are not too difficult to resolve, they can present inconveniences.

4. While a homestead may protect equity to the allowed amount, a creditor attachment may nevertheless prevent a sale or refinancing of the property as it may still constitute a "cloud" on title.

As you can see, the reasons for not declaring a homestead largely relate to the uncertainty about its degree of actual protection. That uncertainty, standing alone, is probably no reason to forego the homestead protection. The wiser approach is to determine whether the homestead will provide greater or lesser protection than having the property titled in some other manner.

Insurance Exemptions

In 1841 the first life insurance exemption statute was enacted. Now every state grants significant exemptions for life insurance from collection by the owner's creditors. In many states, the exemption extends to creditors of the beneficiary. In addition to exemptions for individual life insurance policies, most states provide for exemption of term insurance as well as group life insurance.

States frequently place no limitation on the amount of exempt life insurance. Some states limit the exemption by placing a dollar ceiling on the face amount of the policies held by the insured. In these states, if the face amount exceeds the ceiling, creditors of the insured can reach proceeds which exceed the limitation.

These statutes generally exempt insurance proceeds payable to a qualified beneficiary upon the insured's death. The exemption usually extends to the cash surrender value of the policy as well. Many states also exempt the proceeds which are paid upon

the death of the insured from the beneficiary's creditors.

Exemption of life insurance proceeds is justified on the basis that it affords protection to dependents of the insured. However, some states grant the exemption even if persons other than dependents are beneficiaries.

Tip

> *Although individually-owned life insurance may offer exemption from creditor claims, for tax purposes it may be preferable to establish an irrevocable life insurance trust to own the policies on your life. Review this with your tax advisor.*

Tip

> *If you are subject to creditor claims and you are named beneficiary of an insurance policy, request that the owner of the policy change the beneficiary to a trust*

*to which you are beneficiary, or
alternatively to a spouse or chil-*   *dren not subject to creditor problems.*

Retirement Income and Pension Plans

Federal and state laws exempt from creditor attachment retirement funds paid through public (federal or state government) retirement programs. Hence, payments to former public employees are generally free from creditor attachment. Similarly, all Social Security payments are exempt from all types of legal process.

Tip

*While these retirement funds cannot be attached so as to prevent payment to you, these funds can be attached **once received** and placed, for example, in a general bank account.*

Less clear is whether private retirement programs such as IRAs, Keoughs and employee-sponsored pension programs can be attached by creditors. Many state statutes protect both the principal and/or income of private retirement programs and the applicability of these statutes should certainly be checked in your state. Most cases hold, however, that IRAs, Keoughs and other pension plans are subject to creditor claims.

Congress, when first enacting the pension laws, made some attempt to shield retirement funds from creditors' claims. Nevertheless, there are instances when creditors can successfully reach a debtor's interest in a retirement account.

The best way to approach the topic is to first examine the type retirement account in question, and next consider whether it is a bankruptcy or non-bankruptcy proceeding.

Generally, retirement plans that were protected by the courts were those reasonably designed to provide true retirement benefits in contrast to plans ostensibly established for some other purpose.

Whether a retirement fund will be treated as exempt depends on a number of factors:

1. How large is the accumulation? Excess accumulations beyond what is reasonably required for retirement may endanger the plan.

2. Who administers the plan? When an individual is the sole trustee of his retirement trust, there is greater likelihood of a successful attack then in cases where a third party administers the trust.

3. Are the funds held intact? Frequent distributions or loans from the retirement fund to the individual beneficiary can cause problems.

In essence, a retirement fund will be protected to the extent the account is reasonable as to amount, is administered by an independent third party and is generally held intact rather than treated as personal funds.

ERISA funds are specifically exempted from creditor attachment, and to this extent, preempts state laws since ERISA prohibits the alienation of benefits provided by a qualified plan.

For this reason ERISA plans would normally be protected in a non-bankruptcy situation. On the other hand, IRA's (individual retirement accounts) are not accorded the same protection as ERISA plans and therefore, IRA's can usually be seized by creditors. This is particularly true if the IRA was voluntarily established as opposed to one where it was required by the employer.

What about bankruptcy? Here the law becomes even less clear. It is usually determined that ERISA accounts are not exempt under federal bankruptcy laws although there are several provisions of the bankruptcy code that may allow a debtor a "safe harbor." One is where the pension plan trust is tantamount to a spendthrift trust under state law. Another is by claiming the retirement plan under the general state or federal exemptions generally allowed in bankruptcy.

Because bankruptcy proceedings may endanger pension accounts it is particularly important for a debtor to seek the services of experienced bankruptcy counsel and equally important that counsel know about prior Bankruptcy Court rulings in respect to rights concerning ERISA and similar retirement funds.

Welfare Payments

More than half the states place the most common type of public assistance, aid to families with dependent children, beyond the reach of creditors. Some states grant exemptions for other forms of public assistance such as aid to the blind, the elderly and the disabled. The statutes not only prohibit a creditor from garnishing the state for payments to be made to the debtor, but also exempt the assistance money after it has been paid to the debtor.

Tip

> *In these states, it is recommended that the exempted proceeds be maintained in a separate account and not commingled with non-exempt funds.*

Wages and Other Exempt Income

Most states partially or totally exempt unemployment and workmen's compensation payments.

Surprisingly, and contrary to popular belief, alimony and child support payments generally are not exempt from either the payor's or recipient's creditors, although in some states support payments have a limited exemption.

Both federal and state legislation exempt specified amounts of wage income of a judgment debtor from the reach of creditors by the use of garnishment or other judicial process.

Federal legislation provides a basic wage exemption pursuant to Title III of the Consumer Credit Protection Act (CCPA) and provides some specific exemptions principally related to federal payments and the Employee Retirement Income Security Act (ERISA). Under ERISA, pensions generally cannot be garnished.

Congress has legislated a major exception to these specific federal income exemptions. Pursuant to the Child Support Enforcement Act of 1975, the income exemptions are not applicable as to enforcement of alimony or child support decrees.

Under the federal wage exemption scheme established by CCPA, the maximum part of the aggregate disposable earnings of an individual for any work week that is subject to garnishment may not exceed the lesser of (1) 25% of his disposable earnings for that week or (2) the amount by which his disposable earnings for the week exceeds 30 times the federal minimum hourly wage.

CCPA does permit a greater garnishment to enforce court support orders. "Disposable" earnings are defined as that part of an individual's gross compensation for personal services that remains after deduction of amounts required by law to be withheld.

Although CCPA preempts state garnishment laws that permit greater garnishment than that provided by CCPA, more protective state exemption law, still can apply instead of CCPA.

Under state exemption laws, creditors' access to the debtor's income may be limited further. Certain states, such as Florida and Texas, totally prohibit garnishment of wages. The state wage exemption statutes affect various forms of income, including wages, pensions, and public assistance payments.

Specific income exemptions enacted by each state follow.

STATE INCOME EXEMPTIONS

Exempt

Arizona 50% of earnings for 30 days prior to levy for use of family.

Alabama 30% of weekly disposable income or amount by which disposable earnings per week are in excess of 50 times federal minimum hourly wage.

Alaska Earnings of judgment debtor not to exceed $350 for head of family, $200 for single man for personal services rendered within 30 days preceding levy of execution where necessary to support debtor's family.

Arkansas Wages for 60 days exempt provided statement is filed that wages are less than $200 if single, and $500 for a family. First $25 a week net wages exempt.

California Greater than 50% or portion exempt by federal statute of the earnings of the defendant or judgment debtor received for his personal services rendered at any time within 30 days next preceding the levy of attachment or execution.

Colorado Earnings 70%, 35% if single.

Connecticut Greater amount 75% of disposable earnings per week up to greater of 65% or amount equal to 40 times federal minimum hourly wage.

Delaware Earnings: 90% in New Castle County, 60% in Kent and Sussex, not exempt if self-employed. Liability for balance applies only to necessities of life.

District of Columbia Greater of 75% of disposable earnings per week or amount of disposable earnings per week equal to 30 times federal minimum hourly wage. Withhold by garnishee-employer 90% of first $200 of gross wages, payable in a month in excess of $200 or under $500.

Florida All earnings exempt except for alimony and support payments at discretion of court.

Georgia Greater of 75% of disposable earnings per week or amount by which disposable earnings exceed 30 times the federal minimum hourly wage.

Hawaii 95% of first $100, 90% of next $100, and 80% of gross wages in excess of $200 per month or equivalent per week.

Idaho	Earnings 75% for his personal service rendered within 30 days preceding levy if necessary for use of family supported by his labor; provided that if garnishment be founded upon debt for necessaries, exemption shall not exceed 50% of wages or salary due at time of service of execution or attachment. In no case shall exemption exceed $100 at any one time.
Illinois	Earnings: 85% with minimum of $50 per week if single, or $65 if head of household, and maximum of $200 per week.
Indiana	75% of disposable earnings per week in excess of 30 times federal minimum hourly wage.
Iowa	75% of disposable earnings for week or amount by which disposable earnings exceed 30 times federal minimum hourly wage, whichever is greater. Maximum amount that can be garnished in any year is $250 for each creditor.
Kansas	75% of disposable earnings for week or amount by which disposable earnings exceed 30 times federal minimum hourly wage, whichever is greater. Exemption inapplicable to support orders.
Kentucky	Greater of 75% of disposable income per week or amount by which disposable earnings exceed 30 times federal minimum hourly wage. Exemption inapplicable to support orders.
Louisiana	75% of disposable earnings for any week, but not less than $70 on loans in excess of 10%. Lenders forbidden to use garnishment.
Maine	Greater of 75% of disposable earnings for week or amount by which disposable earnings exceed 10 times federal minimum hourly wage.
Maryland	Wages $150 exempt multiplied by the number of weeks in which said wages were earned or 75% of such wages, whichever is greater; except that in Caroline, Worcester, Kent and Queen Anne counties, exemption for any work week shall be greater of 75% of wages due or 30 times federal minimum wage.
Massachusetts	Wages for personal labor or services exempted from attachment to amount of $125 per week. Exemption of $75 of personal income which is not otherwise exempt by law.

Michigan	Householder with family, 60% exemption with following limitations: On first garnishment, maximum $50 per week for labor of one week. For more than one week's labor, maximum $90 and minimum $60. As to subsequent garnishments for one week's labor, maximum per week is $60 and minimum $24. For a period of more than 16 days, maximum is $60 and minimum $30. Employee, not householder with family, first garnishment 40% exemption with $50 maximum, $20 maximum and $10 minimum.
Minnesota	75% of net wages due at time of attachment, garnishment, or levy or 8 times the number of business days and paid holidays, not greater than 5 per week in the pay period, times the federal minimum hourly wage, whichever is greater. Where debtor has been on relief, exemption for a period of six months from date of return to private employment.
Mississippi	75% of wages or salaries of resident laborer or employee.
Missouri	Greater of (1) 75% of weekly earnings, (2) weekly amount equal to 30 times federal minimum hourly wage or (3) 90% of work week earnings.
Montana	All earnings for 45 days preceding garnishment, limited to 50% exemption.
Nebraska	Greatest of 75% of disposable earnings or amount equal to 30 times federal minimum hourly wage or 85% of disposable earnings if wage earner is head of family.
Nevada	The greater of 75% of disposable earnings or the amount by which disposable earnings exceed 30 times the minimum federal hourly wage.
New Hampshire	Wages for labor performed after service of writ: wages for labor performed before service exempt unless action founded on debt on judgment issued by state court. In such cases wages equal to 50 times federal minimum hourly wage are exempt. Special exemption for small loan law debt.
New Jersey	Earnings 90% if debtor earns $7,500 a year or less. If more than $7,500, garnishee fixed by court.
New Mexico	Greater of 75% of debtor's disposable earnings or of excess of 40 times federal minimum hourly wage rate. Disposable earnings is that part of the debtor's salary remaining after deduction of amounts required to be withheld by law.
New York	Earnings 90%, unless less than $85 per week is earned. Balance is payable as installments.

North Carolina	Earnings 60 days preceding garnishee, if necessary for support of family.
North Dakota	Greater of 75% of debtor's disposable earnings or of excess of 40 times federal minimum hourly wage.
Ohio	Greater of 82 1/2% of the debtor's disposable income or 175 times federal minimum hourly wage. Statutory scheme preempted by Federal Consumer Protection Act.
Oklahoma	Earnings: 75% ninety days; 100% shown to be necessaries for support of family; single man, 75% of wages.
Oregon	Greater of 75% of disposable earnings for week or amounts by which disposable earnings exceed 30 times the federal minimum hourly wage.
Pennsylvania	100% of all wages. Does not apply to support orders of court.
Rhode Island	Earnings: $50 plus salary and wages of dependents; 100% for debtor on relief; and all earnings one year after off-relief.
South Dakota	100% of all earnings within 60 days, if necessary for support of family. However, 15% may be attached for judgment for food, fuel, or medicines.
Tennessee	Wages to 50%, minimum $20, maximum $50 per week; if single, 40%, $17.50 and $40 per week respectively; $2.50 per week addition for each dependent.
Texas	All wages for personal services.
Utah	Married man or head of family: one half of earnings for 30 days prior to levy if his earnings are necessary for family support. Minimum exemption of $50 per month on judgments arising from debts on consumer credit sales greater of 75% disposable earnings per week or 30 times federal minimum hourly wage.
Vermont	75% of disposable earnings for that week or excess of 30 times federal minimum hourly wage, whichever is greater.
Virginia	75% of disposable earnings for that week or excess of 30 times federal minimum hourly wage, whichever is greater. Exemption is inapplicable to court order for support.

Washington
The greater part of 40 times of the state hourly minimum wage or of 75% of disposable earnings of defendant is exempt from garnishment. Disposable earnings means that part of the earnings remaining after deductions of the amount required by law to be withheld.

West Virginia
$20 per week minimum of 80% of wages due or to become due within one year after issuance of execution.

Wisconsin
Greater of 75% of debtor's disposable earnings or excess of 30 times federal minimum hourly wage. Disposable earnings means that part of earnings after deduction of required by law to be withheld. Employees with dependents: basic exemptions, $120 plus $20 per dependent for each 30-day period prior to service of process. Maximum exemption, 75% of income. Employees without dependents, basic exemption of 60% of income for each 30-day period prior to service of process. Minimum $75. Maximum $100.

Wyoming
Judgments on consumer credit sales, home or loan, greater of 75% of disposable earnings or excess over 30 times federal minimum hourly wage. Otherwise 50% of earnings for personal service 60 days before levy if necessary for use of resident family.

Trusts and Joint Tenancies

7

Trusts and joint tenancies are commonly used to protect personal or family assets, particularly real estate, such as the family home, and bank accounts and securities such as stocks and bonds.

A trust is a simple arrangement to understand. In essence, a trust is a plan whereby one party (the trustee) holds assets on behalf of one or more other individuals (the beneficiaries). The party that provides the assets to be administered is the grantor or the donor. The grantor and beneficiaries may be one and the same individual.

The parties to a trust may be individuals, partnerships, corporations or even other trusts. For example, a parent may establish a trust with their children as beneficiaries and a bank as the trustee. The trustee has the fiduciary obligation to administer the trust in accordance with its provisions and by following the "prudent man" rule when investing trust assets.

It is the donor that establishes the terms of the trust. Whether creditors can reach property held in trust, whether as property of the donor or property of the beneficiary, will depend largely on these terms. As you will see as you proceed

Using Trusts to Protect Assets

through this chapter, the issue is largely one of control.

The greater the degree of control retained by the donor (or granted the beneficiary) the greater the likelihood the trust will be an ineffective shield from creditor claims.

There are three principal reasons for setting up a trust:

1. Significant estate and income tax savings,

2. Flexibility in the disposition of assets to suit varying needs of members of the family,

3. Protection of donor's assets against the claims of creditors.

Thus, a trust can provide both asset protection and long-term security for relatives who have neither the inclination or the financial acumen to manage a large, complex estate, thereby protecting family assets from loss through imprudent investments.

Irrevocable Trusts

Trusts are classified as either inter vivos or testamentary trusts. Inter vivos trusts (or living trusts) may be revocable or irrevocable. The testamentary trust is created by the decedent's will and becomes irrevocable upon the decedent's death. The inter vivos trust takes immediate effect.

The irrevocable living trust is the primary trust used for asset protection strategies, although recent changes in tax law have made it possible to realize significant federal income and estate tax savings through the use of an irrevocable living trust, adding to its popularity.

An irrevocable trust can include an outright gift of property to keep the trust property both out of the donor's estate, and also out of the reach of creditors. To be effective however, the trust must be properly structured; i.e., the donor must not have any conditions attached to the trust to indicate the donor has not really parted with the trust property. Thus, the donor cannot reserve the right to revoke the trust, or receive the income, or determine how the trust property or income will be distributed (except as provided in the trust instrument).

The irrevocable living trust, by its very definition, means that you're parting with your property on a permanent basis. In other words, you lose control and ownership of the asset. This may be dangerous unless you have sufficient assets outside the proposed trust to provide for your future anticipated needs. Needless to say, an irrevocable trust should be undertaken only after careful analysis of your needs and resources.

Tip

The protection a trust provides directly relates to the degree to which you have surrendered control over the property transferred to the trust. For example, if you reserve the right to revoke the trust you've made the trust property reachable by your creditors.

An irrevocable trust offers the ultimate in asset protection; since you no longer own the asset transferred to the trust, your creditors cannot reach it in an action against you. If, however, the trust is not revocable, your creditors may be able to reach the property placed in trust. The transfer of the property in trust, of course, must also be such that it cannot be set aside as a transfer in fraud of creditors and thus fail to reach our goal of protecting your property from creditor claims.

Irrevocable Minor's Trust

Gifts in trust to minors are increasingly common, both as a means of creating a child's estate and to minimize federal gift, income and estate taxes payable by the donor. Under the present law, the minor's trust is one of the most useful devices available to (1) shield assets from creditors by transferring them to the donor's children, and, at the same time, reduce the donor's current income tax and estate tax.

The Tax Reform Act of 1986 eliminated a number of popular income splitting techniques, such as Clifford trusts. It is also more difficult to use trusts and custodianships to split family income. For instance, under the new law, custodianships under the Uniform Gift to Minors Act have been adversely affected in that it requires all unearned income in excess of $1,000 (of a child under the age of 14) to be taxed at the rate of the child's parents and thus there is often little tax advantage.

Tip

> *Trusts created under Code § 2503(c) as "Minor's Trust" are a useful vehicle for shifting both wealth and income to younger members of the family. The use of a Minor's Trust is especially valuable after 1987 when the trustee must not only deal with the "under 14" rule, but must also consider how to make maximum use and effect of the trust's 15% income tax rate. Consider the possible tax savings of an irrevocable minor's trust with your tax advisor.*

Properly drafted, the trust agreement can save on taxes and simultaneously shield the assets of the trust from attack by either the donor's (or trustee's) creditors or creditors of the beneficiary.

To be effective as an asset protection tool, the trust agreement must provide for invasion of principal, and cannot impose a substantial restriction on the discretionary powers of the trustee to accumulate income or to invade the trust principal. In some circumstances, a gift of trust income alone, without any distribution of principal, can be made to qualify for the exclusion, to the extent of such income interest. Thus, if the value of the income interest in the property transferred to the trust will exceed the amount of the available exclusions, it is not necessary to give the trustee the same broad discretion over the principal. The trustee need only be given broad discretion as to income and accumulated income. This discretion will not, however, invalidate the trust as an asset protection vehicle.

Despite its possible tax advantages, the minor's trust may not always be advisable. The main problem with a minor's trust arrangement is that the beneficiary will obtain possession of trust property at age 21, whether or not he or she is mature enough to handle a large inheritance at that age.

Life Insurance Trusts

Another popular asset protection trust is the life insurance trust to protect insurance policies from attachment by creditors of the policyowners.

For example, let's assume you have a $1 million life insurance policy — $750,000 in term insurance and $250,000 in whole life. The whole life policy has a $50,000 cash surrender value which will increase over time.

One objective is to make sure that the $50,000 cash value is beyond the reach of your creditors. You also want to be certain that upon your death the insurance proceeds will be paid solely to your wife and children (or other named beneficiaries).

How can you use an insurance trust as an asset protection device?

First, borrow as much as you possibly can against the cash value of your whole life policies. This, of course, is a good strategy whether you use an insurance trust or not, as creditors can reach the surrender value of your policies to the same extent as if it were cash in the bank.

Second, establish a specific trust to receive your insurance policies. You may name your spouse or other trusted individual as trustee. You may designate whomever you choose as beneficiary of the trust. Moreover, since there is no cash value to the insurance at the time of transfer, there would be no gift tax consequences.

While the insurance policies are held in trust you can continue to advance funds to the trustee for purposes of paying the insurance premiums. On the other hand, while the policies are held in trust, your creditors will be unable to reach any cash benefits accumulation under the policies.

You can then arrange for the disposition upon your death. You may, for example, choose to have the proceeds paid directly to your spouse or your children or perhaps administered for them through the same trust or by spillover into a separate trust.

An insurance trust may be either funded or unfunded, revocable or irrevocable, and may be created by either the insured or by another party. In an unfunded insurance trust, either the policy is paid up or the trustor, or another party makes future premium payments.

A revocable life insurance trust involves transferring insurance policies to a trust during the insurer's lifetime. Generally, the insured retains ownership of the policies rather than assigning them to the trust.

Once an insured creates an unfunded revocable life insurance trust, just the life insurance policies are transferred to the trust. The insured remains obligated to pay the insurance premiums. A funded revocable life insurance trust is created when the insured also transfers income-producing property (e.g., cash or securities) from which future premiums on the insurance policies are paid.

Since the trust is revocable, the donor can change the trust provisions during his lifetime, cancel the policies, or cancel the trust. Thus, he retains all rights in the policies during his lifetime. At the donor's death, the trust becomes irrevocable. This gives the donor flexibility to shape the trust to match changing plans and objectives.

In contrast, an irrevocable life insurance trust is created by irrevocably transferring ownership of the policies to the trust. The trust may be funded or unfunded. An unfunded irrevocable trust is created by an irrevocable transfer of only the life insurance policies. Since the trustee of the trust will have no funds with which to pay premiums, the insured or trust beneficiary must pay the premiums.

A funded irrevocable trust is created when transfer is made to the trust of the policies plus income-producing property, the income being used to pay the premiums.

Tip

> *The irrevocable insurance trust serves the useful function of insulating the donor's insurance policies from the claims of creditors and this form of insurance trust rather than the revocable trust should be used for that purpose.*

Revocable Trusts

A revocable (or "nominee") trust generally offers no protection to the donor against attachment of trust assets by the donor's creditors. The donor, by reserving the power to amend or revoke the trust, retains the right to take the assets back from the trust. Therefore, the donor's creditors, in an action against the donor, can compel the donor to revoke the trust and apply the trust assets to satisfy the judgment claims.

Statutes and court rulings vary from state to state but, as a matter of practice, never rely upon a revocable living trust to shield your assets against the claims of creditors. As can be seen from the material that follows, revocable living trusts, at best, offer limited, uncertain asset protection.

Revocable living trusts offer, under certain circumstances, limited exemption from attachment of trust assets. Depending upon applicable state law, trust assets may be protected against the claims of the donor's creditors even though the power to revoke the trust, the right to receive the trust income and other rights and powers have been reserved.

In some states, the donor's creditors can not reach trust assets to satisfy their claims unless the transfer in trust had been made with an intent to defraud the creditors, or the donor retains both a life estate and a general power of appointment as to the remainder; a combination of interests deemed equivalent to substantial ownership of trust assets, creating in essence a trust for the sole benefit of the donor and thus reachable by the donor's creditors.

In several states, statutes provide that a donor who retains an unlimited power of revocation is deemed the absolute owner of the trust property insofar as creditors are concerned. For example, in Ohio a revocable trust is valid as to all persons even though the creator of the trust reserves the requisite powers to amend or revoke, except that any beneficial interest retained by the donor is reachable by his creditors. Similar rulings exist in Alabama, Indiana, Kansas, Michigan, Minnesota and Wisconsin.

Can a donor's creditors claim trust assets upon a donor's death? Most courts hold that a donor's creditors cannot reach the assets of a revocable trust established for others when the donor was solvent. This assumes the debtor neither revoked the trust nor took possession of its assets. If the transfer is made in fraud of creditors it is clear that the creditors may nevertheless assert their claims against the trust.

Other states hold that where the donor reserves beneficial rights under the trust (such as the right to receive income), the donor's creditors may collect their debts after the donor's death out of assets which were payable to the donor, even if the donor did not act fraudulently or was not insolvent when he established the trust.

In yet other jurisdictions creditors are allowed to reach property of a trust over which the donor reserved a life interest. The Bankruptcy Code would also provide creditors the ability to reach trust property when the donor reserves relatively broad powers in his or her own favor.

Assume a situation where a person places property in trust and reserves the right to amend and revoke the trust, or to direct disposition of principal and income and dies. The donors creditors must first look to the debtor's estate to satisfy their claim. If there are not enough assets in the estate, the creditors can then go after those assets owned by the trust over which the owner had such control that he would have been able to use them for his own benefit. Those assets owned by the trust over which the donor had such control at the time of his death as would have enabled the donor to use the trust assets for his own benefit.

It would appear that in order to obtain complete protection of assets against judgment, creditors should transfer ownership of property irrevocably to the trust. Since you no longer own the property, it cannot be attached by your creditors. This would be true as long as the transfer was not made in fraud of your creditors.

Although the revocable living trust offers little asset protection it is still an extremely popular form of trust. The revocable living trust has its most important application in situations where a person seeks to avoid probate after his or her death. By avoiding probate, you'll minimize attorney's fees and court costs, avoid lengthy delays before the beneficiaries can claim their inheritance and eliminate the publicity attendant to the probate process. Just as the revocable living trust offers no protection of assets against the claims of creditors, it offers no tax advantages or disadvantages. All trust incomes, losses and deductions are on the personal tax return of the donor.

Revocable trusts *can* be used effectively in asset protection if, for example, two revocable trusts are set up between husband and wife.

Into the wife's trust, assuming she is the less vulnerable spouse, are placed the family's more valuable assets. Into the husband's trust are placed only a few assets of small value. Even though these are revocable trusts, what happens if the husband, who we shall say for this purpose is a businessman, is sued? Answer: Only the assets within the husband's trust, as a general rule, are now reachable by his creditors. The assets in the wife's trust, as a general rule, are now immunized from the lawsuits against the husband unless, of course, the conveyance to the wife's trust amounts to a "fraudulent conveyance."

Asset protection planning often includes the utilization of the two revocable trusts. Let's examine in greater detail the wife's trust in the foregoing example. The wife could establish the trust. Likewise, the wife would be the beneficiary of the trust. But, as a general rule, the husband may be a co-trustee with the wife over the wife's trust without the assets in the wife's revocable trust vulnerable to attack by the husband's creditors.

Land Trusts

There is a growing trend under which people use a special type of trust called the land trust (frequently known by statute as the Illinois Land Trust, the Florida Land Trust, etc.) as an asset protection device. These trusts are created by state statute and are thus governed by the laws of the states that have adopted land trusts. As a general rule, this type of trust is set up because it offers maximum privacy. The beneficial interest holders of the land trust are not easily discovered because the property may be recorded in the name of a trustee of the trust rather than in the names of the beneficiaries who really hold the equitable interests to the trust property.

From an initial viewpoint at least, such trusts appear to provide protection against lawsuits. However, a primary purpose of a land trust is that of assuring the privacy of those who own the trust. For example, debtors who want to prevent creditors from merely going to a recorder's office to discover what property they have in a particular locale will record their assets in the name of a land trust.

However, a false sense of security accompanies land trusts in that debtors frequently think that such assets are necessarily protected from lawsuits. Once sued, and asked, "Do you have legal or equitable interests in any assets?" You must then, *under penalties of perjury,* disclose that "Yes, I do have a beneficial interest in one or more land trusts," and accordingly, those interests can now be reachable.

The beneficiaries of the trust can best be protected by the way title is held as to the beneficial interest. For example, beneficial interest should be in the wife's name or the husband's name, depending on who is the less vulnerable spouse, or alternatively held by the children when both spouses are vulnerable. Typically with land trusts, the children are named as 100% owners of the beneficial interests in the trust for precisely this reason.

Land trusts create two possible drawbacks: (1) if you decide to refinance or "get a second mortgage," some trustees (particularly institutional trustees) may refuse to execute the mortgage documents, thus temporarily requiring title to come out of the trust into the owner's name until the mortgage can be recorded, and (2) if the trust beneficiary wants to take advantage of a Section 1031 tax-free, like-kind exchange, title must again be taken out of the trust before the real property exchange is completed (since a land trust is an interest in personal property).

Business Trusts

Business trusts have been known for years and their origin can be traced to Massachusetts. Generally speaking, they have the advantage of providing limited liability protection to the certificate holders without the constraints and duties normally imposed upon a corporation. Thus, the business trust can be an excellent asset protection device, if properly used. However, state laws vary greatly and you should investigate the applicable state law to determine the feasibility and potential benefits of a business trust to your asset protection planning.

The most significant characteristic of a business trust, and the most important distinction between a business trust and an ordinary trust, lies in its profit-making function. While an ordinary trust is a tool for the holding and conservation of a particular property with incidental powers of sale and investment vested in its trustee, the business trust is a vehicle for the conduct of a business and the generation of profits from active operations.

In basic terms, a business trust is defined as an association (1) in which trustees hold and own as principals the property, (2) of a business which they manage as trustees, (3) pursuant to an agreement of trust, (4) for the benefit of shareholders who share the profits. In the absence of any one of these features, the association is not a business trust.

Although a business trust has many characteristics of a corporation, and works much like a corporation, the basic distinction between the two is clear: A business trust is created by an agreement of trust, a wholly private transaction between the parties. A corporation, on the other hand, is created by the filing of a certificate or articles of incorporation under a general or special incorporation statute, and thus is chartered by the state.

Clearly, stock ownership in a business trust can be reached by creditors. Thus, like other entities, the ownership interest should be held by the less vulnerable spouse or by the children. In this regard, the business trust offers no special asset protection benefit other than the fact it will be more difficult for creditors to discover who the stockholders happen to be. Another advantage of a business trust is that, unlike other trusts, a business trust can file for bankruptcy.

Disadvantages of the business trust include a tendency by state and federal tax agencies to subject such trusts to the same regulations and taxes imposed on corporations. One additional disadvantage is that in some states the beneficial interest owners may become personally liable for business debts, or at least to the extent they have the power to control managerial decisions.

Tip

A provision in the trust agreement specifically limiting any beneficial interest owner's personal liability and limiting any control over trustees is an effective way to avoid personal liability.

Four Strategies to Improve Trust Protection

Although your trust will be designed both with asset protection and other objectives (taxes, estate planning, etc.) in mind, certain other provisions can greatly increase the effectiveness of any trust as a shield against creditors:

1. Seek reasons for establishing the trust other than protection of assets from future judgment creditors (e.g., to protect assets from demanding children; for estate planning purposes, etc.).

2. Unless the donor resides in a state where creditors cannot reach property in a totally discretionary trust, do not give the trustee absolute discretion to distribute income and principal to the donor alone. The trustee's powers on behalf of the donor should be tightly restricted.

3. Consider adding additional beneficiaries to a trust to protect the donor's interest. So, for example, some statutes provide that a transfer in trust for the use of the donor is void as against creditors. These statutes however, apply only where the donor is sole beneficiary of the trust.

4. If the donor is creating a trust for his or her benefit, consider omitting any type of spendthrift clause. The clause is invalid with respect to the donor and lessens the court's opportunity to find other reasons for the donor's establishment of the trust.

How Jointly Held Title Insulates Property

Owning property jointly with other persons can often be an ideal way to protect certain assets from creditors.

Joint ownership of property is the most popular form of family ownership of property, while at the same time the least understood. More than 80% of all the real estate owned by married couples in the United States is held in joint tenancy. Once you consider joint bank accounts, joint ownership of stocks and bonds, and joint safe deposit boxes it becomes apparent that joint ownership of property is by far the most prevalent form of ownership. Nor is joint ownership of property limited to husbands and wives. It is quite common to see homes, bank accounts, even an automobile owned in joint tenancy by a mother and daughter, by parents and a teenage child, by two business partners, or even by close friends.

Problems most often arise when a creditor of one owner tries to collect its debt by levying on the jointly-owned property. Can the creditor of one joint tenant take the entire property? Can he at least reach the debtor's share of the property? Can the creditor force a sale or a division of the property to satisfy the debt? In other words, need you worry about the creditors of your co-tenant or joint tenant? Can his creditors reach your money in the bank account or your share of the residence? Of equal importance, do your creditors have greater, or less opportunity to reach your share of the property.

In this section we'll examine the rights of one co-tenant or joint tenant against the creditors of another, and the problems a creditor may encounter in levying the jointly-owned property of his debtor.

Three Types of Co-tenancies

When more than one person simultaneously holds title to a property, they're considered co-tenants of that property. Co-tenancy can, however, take one of several legal forms:

● Tenancy in common

● Joint tenancy

● Tenancy by the entirety

The rights of creditors vary widely de-

pending on the type of tenancy as well as the applicable state law as it relates to each form of tenancy. Of course, there are many other factors that can influence the type of tenancy selected, including tax considerations, estate planning and the nature of the property or nature of the relationship between the co-tenants. Technically, there is a fourth type of co-tenancy known as tenancy by partnership, discussed in Chapter 8.

Tenants in Common

Under a tenancy in common each tenant owns a divided interest in the property. Each co-tenant can therefore sell or encumber his share of the property free from interference from his or her co-tenants.

Because a tenant in common holds an interest separate and apart from that of the

co-tenants, his creditors can reach only his interest. Conversely, his interest is not affected by the claims of his co-tenants' creditors, who can reach only the co-tenants interest in the property.

Of more practical importance, an attaching creditor can petition the court to sell the property and thus turn the property into cash by which the claim can be satisfied. Therefore, holding property with a co-tenant under a tenancy in common is not without its potential consequences as you may find yourself owning the property with your co-tenants' creditors. For this reason it is important to select co-tenants who appear free from potential financial problems.

Tip

Should one co-tenant experience financial problems, it is generally best to transfer his or her interest to the remaining co-tenants as such a transfer can usually be supported with less consideration since it represents only a fractional share of the property.

Joint Tenancy

A joint tenancy occurs when property is owned by two or more persons in equal shares with the express declaration that the title is held in joint tenancy. A joint tenancy may be created by the seller conveying to two or more persons, as joint tenants, or by Bone of a present owner conveying to himself and one or more persons as joint tenants.

In most jurisdictions joint tenancy must be created by a written instrument and not by an oral agreement. In the event of simultaneous deaths, the joint tenancy is extinguished and the undivided interest of each tenant is divided as if he or she had survived the other. For instance, the joint property of husband and wife would be divided equally, so that one-half passes through the husband's estate and the other half through the wife's estate.

Joint tenancy conveys to each tenant equal and undivided interest in the property. However, if any one joint tenant conveys his interest, the joint tenancy ends and the parties become tenants in common as to the conveyed interest.

Joint tenancy has one characteristic that distinguishes it from all other forms of ownership: Upon the death of one of the

joint tenants, the surviving tenant or tenants become the sole owners of the entire property by operation of law. The decedent's will has no effect on the disposition of a jointly-held property. In some states, a joint tenancy between a husband and wife is presumed to be tenancy by the entirety. This form of ownership is similar to joint tenancy with a right of survivorship, except neither spouse may sever the tenancy without the other's consent.

A principal disadvantage of joint tenancy is its general inflexibility and the inability of the tenants to dispose of the property by will, except upon the death of the survivor. In addition, since the entire interest in the property passes to the surviving tenant outright, all of it is subject to inclusion in the survivor's estate. This, however, can also be an advantage since the undivided interest of one tenant cannot be seized as readily by his creditors as under a tenancy in common, although holding property as a joint tenant still offers little creditor protection since creditors can nevertheless attach a jointly-held interest and petition the court to "partition" the property, divide its ownership as under a co-tenancy, and then order it to be sold.

Tenants by the Entirety

Spouses may establish a tenancy by the entirety as a special form of joint tenancy. Its origins can be traced to earlier English law when property was transferred to

husband and wife together. At that time man and woman, as a result of marriage, for legal purposes, were treated as a unification of the two people, so that their ownership of property (usually real estate) was not regarded as being owned by the two individuals, but by the "unity," or by the "entirety." Under this concept the property is owned not by two people but rather by "the unity" created when the parties are married, and who then take title as a "single" person.

Because of this entirety or "unity" concept, neither party, acting alone, can legally transfer his or her interest in the property held by the entirety, and on the death of either party, the survivor would own the whole property. In this respect, tenancy by the entirety works similarly to a joint tenancy. The tenancy in the entirety operates until both parties agree to a transfer or until the marriage is dissolved by law or by the death of one of the parties.

Presently, approximately one-half the states recognize tenancy by the entirety. The laws applicable to this form of ownership vary from state to state with certain basic similarity in concept and elements. Many states, however, have actually abolished tenancy by the entirety on the theory that it is out-moded and does not reflect the present-day attitude that husband and wife are individuals, notwithstanding their marriage relationship.

In many states that recognize tenancy by the entirety, a presumption often exists that when husband and wife take property as joint tenants, they instead take ownership as tenants by the entirety. To eliminate this presumption, if your intentions are to own the property in true joint tenancy, the title should read as "joint tenants and not as tenants by the entirety." It is important to consult your local state law to determine the full implications of various forms of property ownerships, and to have local counsel carefully review deeds of conveyance.

Does property held as tenants by the entirety offer adequate creditor protection? The answer depends entirely upon state laws. Unfortunately, in most states there is no legal distinction between joint tenancies and tenancies by the entirety. Therefore, a creditor of one spouse can reach that spouse's interest in the "entirety" property,

often forcing a sale of the property (commonly the family home) and satisfying its claims by seizing one-half the proceeds.

But, in some states, holding title as tenants by the entirety offers substantial protection. In other states the property remains relatively protected if the wife (but not the husband) incurs debts because the husband is presumed to have the rights to income and possession of the premises.

There are limitations to a tenancy by the entirety as an asset protection device. First is the question of what happens if the husband or wife should later divorce. Unless the property is transferred to a third party the property will necessarily be transferred to one spouse or the other and the property no longer protected should the property go to the spouse with creditors.

Secondly, it may be true that a creditor cannot seize a property so held, nevertheless the creditor may cloud title to the property by filing a judgement or attachment against one party or the other. This may prevent remortgaging or a sale of the property.

Third, one spouse may die and the property would automatically vest in the surviving spouse. If the surviving spouse has creditors, these creditors would have clear claim to the equity in the property.

Fourth, we have the issue of safety of the proceeds should the property be sold or refinanced. If the proceeds are to be divided between the spouses then creditors of either spouse would have the right to reach and apply these proceeds.

Finally, the bankruptcy of either spouse may cause complications as the trustee in a bankruptcy may force a sale of the property. It is important to point out that the trustee only receives the one-half undivided interest of the bankrupt spouse and therefore can only sell that same interest. This has little marketable value because the interest remains subject to the survivorship rights of the other spouse. This highlights why a husband and wife as tenants by the entirety should *never* file bankruptcy simultaneously. By staggering the bankruptcies, neither the wife's nor the husband's trustee gains full title to the property. With staggered bankruptcies it should be possible for a third party (such as a friend or relative) to pur-chase the interest of a bankrupt spouse for nominal value.

Selecting Joint Tenancy or Tenancy by the Entirety

The tenancy by the entirety and the joint tenancy both create a right of survivorship. On the death of either owner, the survivor owns the entire property. However, there are important differences between the two.

First, a joint tenancy may be held by any number of persons, of any relationship, while a tenancy by the entirety may be held only by husband and wife.

Second, any one of the joint tenants, by transferring his ownership to a third party, can terminate the joint tenancy. A tenancy by the entirety may not be transferred unless both parties agree, and may not be severed except by dissolution of marriage, or by the death of one of the spouses, or by agreement between husband and wife.

The right of a surviving spouse to own the entire property on the death of a spouse is one of the major advantages of holding property by the entirety. The property passes to the surviving spouse. It becomes hers or his alone. It avoids probate. It is not subject to the claims of creditors of the deceased spouse (unless the property itself was pledged as collateral or security, such as a mortgage). The surviving spouse is then free to dispose of the property, regardless of any provision to the contrary in the will of the deceased spouse, and free of any claims against the deceased spouse.

In the event both spouses die simultaneously, the property would be distributed as if it was owned by tenants in common; one-half of the property would pass to the husband's estate and the other half to the wife's estate.

But which form of tenancy offers better protection against creditors?

To better understand the rights of creditors under the various types of tenancies we must often look beyond state laws and investigate whether the debtor (or joint tenant or co-tenant) is alive or deceased at the time the creditor attempts to levy on the property.

Under a joint tenancy, a creditor seeking to satisfy a debt may attach the debtor's interest in property held in a joint tenancy if the debtor/joint tenant is alive at the time of the attachment.

The general legal rule followed by courts is that during the life of a joint tenant, that joint tenant's undivided interest can be reached by his creditors. The theory is that each joint tenant is able to sell or transfer his interest during his life, thus voluntarily severing the joint tenancy between himself and his co-tenants. That sale creates a tenancy in common between the buyer and the other co-tenants. Since each joint tenant can sell or otherwise freely transfer his interest, his creditors should be able to reach that same interest to satisfy a debt owed to creditors by the joint tenant. The creditor's attachment on the joint tenancy creates the same result obtained when a joint tenant's interest is sold. The joint tenancy between the debtor and his co-tenants is destroyed and the creditor becomes a tenant in common with the other co-tenants. The other co-tenants remain joint tenants among themselves free of the creditor's claim.

The law is not as uniform in regard to tenancies by the entirety. As a general rule, if the husband and wife are jointly liable on a debt, the property they hold as tenants by the entirety may be attached during their lifetime and sold to satisfy their debt. However, if only the husband or only the wife is individually liable on a debt, the creditor usually will not be allowed to seize that property.

Except in those states where tenancy by the entirety has been abolished substantially or modified, creditors of the wife may not attach the property and have it sold. Since the wife herself is not allowed to sell her interest in a tenancy by the entirety, her creditors gain no greater rights and will likewise not be allowed to sell it. In effect, the wife's interest in the property is insulated from the claims of her individual creditors during her lifetime.

Except in certain states, such as Massachusetts, where special protection is given by law to a principal residence or other property held under a tenancy by the entirety, a creditor of the husband may place a lien or attachment on the property since the husband has the sole right to possession during his life. However, as a general rule, the property will not be sold to satisfy the husband's debt so long as the wife is alive.

The rights of creditors can dramatically change once the debtor is deceased.

One of the key characteristics of the joint tenancy with rights of survivorship is that the surviving tenant owns the whole property after the death of his joint tenant. In other words, by operation of law, the joint tenancy ceases to exist upon the death of the joint tenant.

One consequence of this characteristic of joint tenancy is that the creditors of a deceased joint tenant may not satisfy their debts from the jointly-held property. The theory behind this is that the property no longer belongs to the joint tenant's estate, but passes as the sole property of the surviving joint tenants. In other words, the creditors cannot reach the joint property because there's "nothing" to reach. Tenants by the entirety enjoy this same "survivorship" feature.

Because a creditor's rights against a debtor under a joint tenancy (or tenancy by the entirety) terminate upon death of the debtor, it can be seen that an attachment during the debtor's lifetime has little value unless it can be liquidated through a forced sale of the property, a result not always easily accomplished under state laws.

Although, as a general rule, a creditor cannot reach the jointly-owned property upon the death of a debtor/joint tenant, there are three recognized exceptions to this rule:

First, if the joint tenancy was created to defraud the creditors it would be deemed a fraudulent conveyance and would be set aside.

A second exception applies in those states that have specific laws regarding creditors' rights against joint property. South Dakota, for example, has a law that allows a creditor to sue a surviving joint tenant for the debts of a deceased joint tenant, and the creditor may reach the joint property to the extent of the deceased joint owner's contribution. Washington also seems to take the position that a joint tenancy will not cause a creditor to lose his rights. But, these states are definitely in the minority.

Third, to the extent that the jointly-held property is subject to federal or state taxes, the surviving joint tenant (or tenant by the entirety) will still own the property but the property will be subject to the payment of taxes. In fact, a lien (a legal attachment) automatically attaches to all property that is subject to tax in the deceased's estate. If there's not enough money to pay the tax out of other property, the jointly-held property may be sold to pay the tax.

The right of a creditor to reach jointly-held property is generally more restricted if the debtor has not filed for bankruptcy. Once in bankruptcy, the creditor may have greater rights. The Federal Bankruptcy Code has established special rules for joint tenancy when one of the joint tenants declares bankruptcy.

Once a person becomes subject to bankruptcy proceedings, all his property comes under the jurisdiction of the court and becomes the property of the "trustee" in bankruptcy. This includes interests as a joint tenant, tenant in common, or tenant by the entirety. Under the Bankruptcy Code, the trustee in bankruptcy may sell the property of the bankrupt co-tenant, regardless of the form of co-tenancy and take the proceeds of the share of the bankrupt co-tenant. The non-bankrupt co-tenant must promptly claim his share of the proceeds of the commonly-held property before these assets are applied to satisfy the bankrupt's debts.

Should the non-bankrupt co-tenant be the true "owner" of jointly-held property in which the bankrupt is his co-tenant, he must prove to the court that his share of the commonly-held property should not be subject to the bankruptcy proceedings which could prove quite difficult.

Tip

> *Co-tenants, such as husband and wife, should never declare bankruptcy at the same time. This*

> *would give the trustee(s) full title to the entire property. If each co-tenant files bankruptcy at a different time, the respective trustees can only sell a fractional share of the property and therefore the property may be re-acquired at a bargain price.*

Joint Bank Accounts

Joint bank accounts between husband and wife, other members of the family or even between two unrelated parties engaged in a business are quite common. It is important to realize the rights of creditors of one of the joint tenants in the event the creditor obtains a judgment against that joint tenant. The central question is whether a creditor of one of the account holders may attach the funds in the jointly-held account to satisfy the debt? Is the creditor entitled to only one-half of the funds in the account or can he attach the entire account? Can the creditor do so if the debtor is the non-contributing co-tenant or if the debtor is only an account holder in name without having contributed any money to the account? The answers to these questions depend upon applicable state law and the specific circumstances of the case.

In many states the law holds that each

tenant of a joint bank account has a "vested" interest in the account. A vested interest is one which legally belongs to a person, providing in effect an absolute ownership. Even in the absence of a specific state law, a court may rule that a creditor who has obtained a judgment against one of the joint tenants now stands in the position of the joint tenant and is able to withdraw the funds in the account just as the joint tenant himself is able to do.

Tip

> *Because jointly-held bank accounts may be subject to attachment to satisfy the debt of one joint tenant, it is advisable to use these accounts only for small sums of money such as a checking account.*

Protecting Community Property

Community property laws, dividing property equally between husband and wife, have now been adopted by nine states: California, Arizona, Nevada, New Mexico, Texas, Louisiana, Washington, Idaho and Wisconsin.

The community property laws, originating from Spanish law, have undergone considerable change in these states, and the laws within these jurisdictions are quite different.

In non-community property states, or common law states, the question of what property a creditor of the husband or wife

may reach to satisfy the creditor's debt is comparatively simple. If the debt is owed by the husband, his property may be reached. If the debt is owed by the wife, her property may be reached. If husband and wife are both liable on the debt, and the liability is joint and several, judgment can be obtained against either or both and the property of either or both, may be reached by execution. In other words, the fact that two individuals are married does not directly affect either their liability for obligations incurred, or the property that may be reached by their creditors. To this extent marital status has no consequence in common law states.

In a community property state, the fact that two individuals are married is of key importance in determining, first, who is liable for the debt, and second, what property may be reached after a creditor obtains judgment.

When a married person in a community property state incurs a debt, it must first be determined whether the debt is that particular individual's separate obligation, a community (or joint) obligation, or an obligation of the other spouse because the contracting party was acting as the spouse's agent.

Therefore, in community property states the following questions need to be answered:

1. Is the debt a separate debt or community (joint) debt?

2. Is the creditor attempting to reach community property or separate property? If the property is community property, is the creditor attempting to reach all the property or only the interest of the debtor spouse?

3. Is the claim one that arose before, during, or after the marriage?

Generally, property that one of the spouses brings to the marriage continues to be his or her separate property during marriage. Gifts and bequests of property to one spouse during the marriage are also the separate property of that spouse, as is inherited property. All other property is community property, including that which is earned by either spouse during the marriage. Commingling of separate property usually converts it to community property. There is also a general presumption that property obtained by either spouse during the marriage is community property. Earnings of a spouse during the marriage are generally community property, but are sometimes treated differently than other community property when creditors of the other spouse attempt to reach them to satisfy a debt of the other spouse.

More difficult to answer is the question of whether a spouse's interest in the community property can be taken to satisfy a spouse's separate debts. Since a spouse does not have the right to withdraw his or her interest in the community property and to make it separate property, in absence of divorce or separation, there should be no right to have the community property partitioned.

The distinction between separate and community property is reasonably clear from the statutes and case law of all community property jurisdictions. The same cannot be said of community debts and separate debts. Except for New Mexico, no other jurisdiction has statutes specifically defining separate and community debts.

Obligations incurred prior to the marriage or after a separation or divorce are consistently treated as the separate obligation of the spouse incurring the debt. On the other hand, debts incurred during the marriage are community obligations.

If the debt arises from a contract made on behalf of the community or if the activity giving rise to an obligation was designed to benefit the community, the presumption is that it is a community obligation (if it was incurred during marriage by either spouse).

A creditor's ability to reach marital property is not affected by the purpose for which a spouse contracts. Whether a spouse contracts for individual benefit or for the benefit of both marital partners, is irrelevant in determining the liability of marital property for debts of either spouse.

California, Texas and Idaho do not recognize the community/separate debt distinction. In those states debts are attributed to spouses individually or jointly, as the case may be. Louisiana and Nevada are community property jurisdictions whose community property laws may differ significantly from those of the other states. This underscores the need to be familiar with the specific laws of your state if it has community property.

A basic concept of community property law is one of marital effort. Property acquired by the efforts of either spouse during marriage is community property. Property acquired before marriage or acquired afterward by gift or inheritance is the separate property of that spouse. This is a good general rule to follow.

Under more modern community property statutes, both spouses have the power to obligate the community property for their individual contracts. On the other hand, with the exception of the "necessaries" of life, neither spouse may unilaterally obligate the separate property of a non-contracting spouse for debts of the spouse who contracts. Of course, where a debt is a joint obligation of husband and wife, the community property together with the separate property of the respective spouses, will be liable for the debt.

Joint liability can be readily established in marriage. For example, where one spouse pays bills of the other spouse, that spouse may be held jointly liable for subsequent debts incurred by the other spouse. By making even a single payment, one spouse grants apparent authority to the other spouse to contract joint debts.

Tip

Spouses seeking to avoid joint liability on marital debts should take precautionary steps. For example, a wife who wishes to avoid liability for her husband's contracts should make clear to the husband, and immediately to the seller if she is billed for the debt, that her husband acted without her authority or consent. If she desires to pay that debt in full or in part, she should inform the seller that her payment does not constitute authority for her husband to make future contracts for which she will assume obligation.

IRREVOCABLE TRUST

Whereas there is about to be or will be conveyed to

of

, as Trustees, certain real estate and real properties located in the Commonwealth of Massachusetts.

Now Therefore,   the said Trustees, hereinafter referred to jointly as the Trustee (if there are more than one Trustee) and in the masculine gender, does hereby declare and acknowledge that he will hold, manage, and dispose of said real estate and all other property, grant, conveyed, assigned or transferred at any time hereafter to him, as Trustee hereunder together with the proceeds thereof, all agreeably to the provisions of this instrument upon the following terms, conditions and trusts for the uses and purposes and with the powers as hereinafter more fully set forth and none other:

ARTICLE I.

NAME

This Trust shall be designated and known as the   and under that name the Trustee shall, as far as practicable, conduct all business and execute all written instruments in the performance of this Trust.

ARTICLE II.

DURATION

This Trust shall endure for the term of twenty-one (21) years after the death of the survivor of any person name herein. This provision is to be construed as a part of and as a limitation upon the duration of this Trust.

ARTICLE III.

RECORDING

A.   This Declaration of Trust shall be recorded with the Registry of Deeds above the first written and may be recorded in all other registries where any realty acquired by the Trust may be located.

B.   Any and all other instruments altering, amending or adding to this Trust or terminating same or the resignation of a Trustee or the appointment of a Trustee to fill a vacancy or otherwise affecting this instrument shall also be so recorded and until so recorded, such instrument(s) shall be ineffectual.

ARTICLE IV.

PURPOSE

The purpose of this Trust is to deal in and with, buy, purchase, own, acquire, hold, exchange, convey, sell, lease, sublease, rent mortgage, pledge, encumber, hypothecate, survey, improve, divide, subdivide, plan, develop for purposes of sale or otherwise, build, construct, alter, remodel, establish, operate, conduct, maintain or otherwise dispose of either as principal, agent or broker, land and real estate of every kind, nature and description and all kinds of personal or mixed property including, without limiting the generality of the foregoing, machinery, boats, chattel mortgages, real mortgages, negotiable and non-negotiable instruments, securities, choses in action, and other obligations: to do and perform all things needful and lawful for carrying same out.

ARTICLE V.

TRUSTEE – TITLE

A.   The Trustee shall have the legal title to the Trust property and Trust funds. The Trustee shall have absolute control, management, and disposition thereof and shall likewise have absolute control and management of all business of the Trust. The enumeration of specific powers hereinafter shall not be construed in any way as limiting the general powers intended to be conferred upon the Trustee.

B.   Upon the appointment of any succeeding Trustee, the title to the Trust shall thereupon and without the necessity of any conveyance by vested in said succeeding Trustee. Reference herein to the Trustee shall mean the Trustee for time being acting hereunder.

ARTICLE VI.

TRUSTEE – GENERAL

The Trustee shall hold all Trust property and Trust funds, hereafter call the Trust "res" now or hereafter held by the Trustee hereunder in Trust for the purposes with powers and subject to the limitations herein for the benefit of the beneficiaries, and it is hereby expressly declared that a trust and not a partnership is hereby created; that neither the

Trustee nor the beneficiaries shall ever be personally liable hereunder as partners or otherwise, but that for all debts and obligations the Trustee shall be liable as such to the extent of the Trust "res" only and in all contracts or instruments creating liability, it shall be expressly stipulated that the beneficiaries shall not be liable and this Declaration of Trust be referred to; no bond will ever be required of the original Trustee or one appointed as hereinafter provided.

ARTICLE VII.

TRUSTEE – POWERS

The Trustee shall have the absolute control, management and disposition of the Trust property as if he were the absolute owner thereof, free from the control of the beneficiaries, and, without the following enumeration limiting the generality of the foregoing or of any item in the enumeration, with full power and uncontrolled discretion, subject only to the limitations and conditions hereof, at any time and from time to time with without the necessity of applying to any court or the beneficiaries hereunder for leave to do so:

A.   The Trustee hereunder, including any successor Trustee or Trustees, in addition to and not in limitation of all common law and statutory authority, shall have power with regard to both real and personal property constituting the Trust "res" and any part thereof as follows:

1.   To take, hold, possess, manage, operate, improve, protect, preserve, maintain, insure, remove, store, transport, repair, rebuild, modify, and/or improve the same;

2.   To buy, receive, lease, let, grant options, accept or otherwise acquire the same;

3.   To hold any Trust property in the name of a nominee without the disclosure of the Trust;

4.   To borrow money with or without security, to mortgage, pledge, hypothecate, quitclaim or otherwise encumber the same;

5.   To convey, transfer, sell, in whole or in part at public or private sale, with or without consideration, to donate, to give away, to contract or agree for the acquisition, disposal or encumbrances of the same or any property whatsoever and wheresoever situated;

6. To invest and reinvest the funds of the Trust in securities or properties although of a kind or in an amount which ordinarily would not be considered suitable for investment;

7. To exchange property for other property;

8. To determine what shall be charged or credited to income and what to principal notwithstanding any determination by the courts;

9. To determine who are the distributees hereunder and the properties in which they shall take;

10. To make payments of principal or income, and otherwise to make distribution or divisions of principal hereunder, in property in kind, at values determined by him;

11. To decide and determine whether or not to make deductions from income for depreciation, obsolescence, amortization or waste, and if so, in what amount;

12. To pay, compromise, or contest any claim or other matter directly or indirectly affect this "res";

13. To institute, prosecute, defend, compromise, arbitrate and/or dispose of legal, equitable or administrative hearings, actions, suits, attachments, arrest, evictions, ejectments, distresses or other proceedings, or otherwise engage in litigation;

14. To employ, or engage the services of and obtain the advice of counsel and to rely thereon;

15. To appoint and employ such other persons, agents, brokers, managers, appraisers, arbitrators, accountants, advisors and/or attorneys in fact as he may deem advisable;

16. To rely upon the opinion or advice of any statement or computation by any attorney, counsel, appraiser, surveyor, engineer, broker, auctioneer, accountant, or other person deemed by him competent, whether or not disinterested or a Trustee or agent of this Trust;

17. To fix and pay compensation of persons designated, appointed, employed, hired by the Trustee under paragraphs 13, 14, 15 and 16; and the Trustee shall not be answerable or responsible for the acts and faults of any such person or persons;

18. To make, execute, acknowledge and deliver all instruments in his opinion necessary and proper to convey the Trust "res" or any part thereof or any

interest therein or in any way relating to or affecting the same or any part thereof or to carry out any of the powers herein contained;

19. Generally to do all the things in relation to the Trust "res" as if the Trustee was absolute owner of the Trust "res" and this Trust has not been executed;

20. Any of the foregoing or any part of the foregoing may be for a period of time which exceeds the probable duration or term of this Trust; and

21. To construe any of the provisions of the Declaration of Trust and to act on any such construction, and this construction of the same and any action taken in good faith pursuant thereto shall be final and conclusive on all parties in interest.

B. All such divisions and decisions made by the Trustee in good faith shall be conclusive on all parties at interest.

C. The exercise of any power herein or hereunder shall not require the approval of any Court.

D. In no case shall any party dealing with the said Trustee in relations to said premises, or to whom said premises or any part thereof shall be conveyed, transferred, contracted to be sold, leased or mortgaged by the said Trustee, be obliged to see to the application of any purchase money, rent or money borrowed or advanced on said premises, or be obliged to see that the terms of this Trust have been complied with, or be obliged to inquire into the necessity or expedience of any act of said Trustee, or be obliged or privileged to inquire into any of the terms of said Trust; and every person relying upon or claiming under any such conveyance or instrument:

1. That at the time of the delivery thereof, the Trust created by this Declaration or any amendment thereof.

2. That such conveyance or instrument was executed in accordance with the terms, conditions, and limitations contained in the Declaration or any amendment thereof.

3. That said Trustee was duly authorized and empowered to execute and deliver every such instrument, and

4. If the conveyance is made to or by a successor in Trust, that such successor in Trust has been properly appointed and is fully vested with all the title, estate, rights, powers, authorities, duties, and obligations of the predecessor in Trust.

178

ARTICLE VIII.

<u>BANKING</u>

A.   The Trustee, or any succeeding Trustee from time to time hereunder, shall have the right to deposit monies in any banking institution, and without limiting the inherent rights of a Trustee, with the following powers:

1.   To endorse for credit to the account of the Trust, any check, draft, note, bill of exchange or other negotiable instrument for the payment of money, or

2.   To cause the same to be endorsed for such purpose by rubber stamp;

3.   To disburse funds under deposit by check, draft, or otherwise upon the signature of the said Trustee or his successor without any obligation of inquiry on the part of the banking institution as to the circumstances of the issue or reason for payment;

4.   To certify the correctness of the balance of the Trust with said banking institution; and

5.   To designate a signatory or signatories on any checking account.

B.   The said banking depository is authorized and directed to pay, certify, apply or otherwise honor or charge to the account of the Trust, without inquiry and without regard to the application of the proceeds thereof, checks, drafts, notes, bills of exchange, and other instruments or orders for the payment, transfer, withdrawal of money for whatever purpose and to whomsoever payable, including those drawn to the individual order of the Trustee.

C.   Checks by a former Trustee which would have been valid but for the termination of his authority by death, removal, or otherwise, and checks drawn by the Trustee payable to himself, shall be conclusively deemed to be valid in favor of any person who shall have had prior valid dealings with such Trustee and who shall have had no actual notice of such termination.

ARTICLE IX.

<u>TRUSTEE DEGREE OF CARE</u>

A.   In dealing with the Trust "res" and management thereof, the Trustee shall not be held to the usual standard of care for Trustees but only to the standard of care of ordinary individuals dealing with their own property and having due regard to reasonable business and speculative chances with the ultimate view of a general increase by means of frequent or otherwise turnings or conversions, and his judgment shall not be subject to review except when dishonestly formed.

B.   The Trustee shall not be liable for any error or judgment or mistake of law, or for any loss arising out of any investment or for any act or omission in the execution of this Trust, as long as he acts in good faith, nor shall he be personally liable for the acts or omissions of any agent or attorney appointed by or acting for him; the Trustee shall not be liable for anything except his own personal and willful misfeasance or fraud.

ARTICLE X.

TRUSTEE – LIABILITY

The Trustee shall have no power or authority to enter into any contract or agreement which shall bind or affect any beneficiary personally or call upon him for the payment of any money whatsoever, but the Trustee shall be entitled to indemnity against any and all liabilities either in contract or tort, which he may incur or to which he may be subject, out of the Trust "res".

ARTICLE XI.

TRUSTEE – COMPENSATION

The Trustee shall receive reasonable compensation for his services hereunder.

ARTICLE XII.

ACCOUNT OF TRUSTEE

The Trustee shall render each year an account of his administration of the Trust to the beneficiaries, whose written approval of such an account shall, as to all matters and transactions stated therein or shown thereby be final and binding upon all persons (whether in being or not) who are then or may thereafter become entitled to share in either the principal or the income of this Trust.

ARTICLE XIII.

BENEFICIARIES

The beneficiaries (herein sometimes referred to as either beneficiary or beneficiaries) are as indicated below along with their respective interests in the said Trust:

%

%

ARTICLE XIV.

RESTRICTIONS ON BENEFICIARIES

The interest of the beneficiaries hereunder, either as to income, interest or principal shall not be anticipated, alienated, or in any other manner assigned by any beneficiary and also shall not be subject to any legal or equitable process, bankruptcy proceedings, or the attachment, interference or control by or of creditors of any beneficiary or of any others.

ARTICLE XV.

INTEREST OF BENEFICIARIES

No title, interest or estate in any lands, buildings or other property held by the Trustee at any time hereunder is to vest in the beneficiaries, the interest of the beneficiaries being equitable; the beneficiaries shall have no right to call for any partition or distribution during the continuance of the Trust; and the sole right, claim and interest of the beneficiaries shall be in the obligation of the Trustee hereunder to hold, manage, apply, dispose of the Trust "res" and account for the income and proceeds thereof in the manner provided for herein. A Trustee may without impropriety be a beneficiary (provided that he is not the sole beneficiary) and exercises all the rights of a beneficiary and the powers of a Trustee.

ARTICLE XVI.

DEALINGS WITH TRUSTEE AND/OR BENEFICIARIES

A. Any Trustee, beneficiary or agent of this Trust or any firm trust, corporation, concern, or estate in which he is interested as a member, trustee, director, officer, beneficiary, shareholder, agent, fiduciary, or otherwise may, when acting in good faith sell or lease to, buy or lease from, contract with, and otherwise deal with this Trust as freely and effectually as though no interest or fiduciary relation existed; and the Trustee hereunder shall have power to exercise or concur in exercising all powers and discretions given to him hereunder or by law, not withstanding that he may have a direct or indirect interest, personally or otherwise, in the mode, result, or effect of exercising such powers or discretions.

B. Without limiting the generality or effect of the foregoing paragraph of this Article, it is hereby provided that, if a conveyance or transfer is made by the Trustee to himself or to any transferee who is in any way interested in this Trust or in whom the

Trustee is interested, directly or indirectly, it shall be conclusively presumed in favor of all persons (other than the Trustee and such transferee) dealing with the property so conveyed or transferred or claiming under such conveyance or transfer that the same has been made in good faith, for adequate consideration, and in accordance with the powers contained in this instrument, and is in all respects valid and proper.

ARTICLE XVII.

DIVIDENDS

The Trustee shall declare dividends from the net income or profit of the Trust "res" for the beneficiaries annually or more often, if convenient to the Trustee, or if the income and profits accumulated in the discretion of the Trustee justified a dividend to be declared, and his decision as to the amount of the dividends shall be final; the Trustee may make distribution to the beneficiaries of any uninvested capital at any time as said Trustee may in his judgment decide, but nothing herein contained shall impair or limit the rights or powers of the Trustee to reserve such sum or sums as he may deem necessary to pay debts, expenses and obligations of the Trust whether due and payable or future or contingent.

ARTICLE XVIII.

PAYMENTS

If payment of income or principal hereunder are due to be made to a person, who is a minor, or who, in the opinion of the Trustee, is not competent or able carefully and properly to handle the same, then said Trustee may in his discretion make such payments in whole or in part for one or more of the following purposes:

A. To the legal guardian or conservator of such person;

B. Expend the same for the comfort, support, education and happiness of such person or pay the same to some person or persons to be expended for such purposes;

C. Accumulate the same for his benefit, but not for a longer period than the life of the last survivor of any person named herein and twenty-one years thereafter, for distribution at such time or times as the Trustee may deem expedient;

D. Reimburse any persons who may have expended money for the comfort, support, education and happiness of any beneficiary hereunder, the same to be wholly within the discretion of the Trustee and his decisions to whether money was so spent to be final.

ARTICLE XIX.

DISTRIBUTION

Upon determination of this Trust, the Trust "res", after payment of all outstanding obligations or liabilities and indemnifying the Trustee for any outstanding obligation or liability, shall be turned over to the beneficiaries as tenants in common; if said termination or dissolution is by act of law, then the beneficiaries shall hold the Trust "res" as tenants in common.

ARTICLE XX.

RESIGNATION OF TRUSTEE

A.   The Trustee hereunder may resign by a written instrument signed, acknowledged and recorded as provided in ARTICLE III "ante".

B.   In the event of any vacancy occurring in the office of Trustee as a result of the death, resignation or inability of a Trustee to serve, or otherwise, such vacancy shall be filled by a majority of the remaining Trustees, and if same are unable to achieve a majority decision as to whom shall be selected then by a majority of the remaining Trustees and such of the Beneficiaries of the Trust as are of full age and legal capacity, and if there are none, by any court of proper jurisdiction. Except in the case of appointment by court, any such appointment shall be in writing, duly signed by the successor Trustee, and acknowledged before a notary public, and recorded as provided in ARTICLE III "ante".

C.   Upon the failure by a majority of the beneficiaries (of full age and legal competence) named and designated in this Trust as provided in the preceding paragraph to appoint a successor Trustee within thirty (30) days of the recording of the resignation of the then Trustee, or within thirty (30) days after the death or inability of the then Trustee to act, then the Probate Court of the County above first written or any other Probate Court of competent jurisdiction in the Commonwealth of Massachusetts upon application of the Beneficiaries and after such notice, if any, as the court may direct, may fill such vacancy and any such Trustee may be required by the court to give bond with or without sureties for the performance of his duties as Trustee, or may be exempt from the giving of such bond; his appointment shall be recorded as provided in ARTICLE III "ante".

D.   Upon the recording of the appointment of a successor Trustee, whether appointed by a majority of the Trustees and/or beneficiaries or by a Probate Court of competent jurisdiction, such succeeding Trustee shall become vested with title to the Trust "res" and shall have with respect thereto all and the same powers as the original Trustee hereunder, except that said successor Trustee shall not be liable for any acts performed or committed by a prior Trustee.

ARTICLE XXI.

TERMINATION AND AMENDMENT

      A.   The Trustee may terminate this Trust at any time by the sale of the "res" and turning over the proceeds thereof to the shareholders hereunder provided heretofore.

      B.   The Trustee may alter, amend or terminate this Declaration with the consent of a majority of the beneficiaries except that no alteration or amendment may be made which shall extend the time of the Trust beyond the term herinbefore fixed.

      C.   The instrument setting forth such alteration, amendment or termination shall be executed and acknowledged by the Trustee, assented to in writing by a majority of the beneficiaries and recorded and provided in ARTICLE III "ante". Any such instrument so executed, acknowledged and recorded shall be conclusive of the existence of all facts and of compliance with all prerequisites necessary to the validity of such alteration, amendment or termination in favor of all persons dealing with the title to the Trust "res" or any part thereof or affecting the rights of third person.

ARTICLE XXII.

COPIES AND CERTIFICATES BY TRUSTEE

      A.   Any person, individual or corporation transacting business with the Trustee hereunder may accept a duplicate or copy of this Declaration or any part thereof or of any amendment hereto, duly acknowledged or certified by the Trustee before a Notary Public or Justice of the Peace, as a true copy hereof.

      B.   Every contract, deed, mortgage, lease and other instrument or document executed by any person appearing from instruments or certificates so filed for record to be a Trustee hereunder shall be conclusive evidence in favor of every person relying thereon or claiming thereunder that at the time of the delivery thereof this Trust was in full force and effect and that the execution and delivery of such instrument were duly authorized by the Trustee.

      C.   Any person dealing with the Trust property or the Trustee may always rely on a certificate signed by any person appearing from instruments or certificates so filed for record to be a Trustee hereunder as to whom are the Trustee or beneficiaries hereunder or as to the existence or non-existence of any fact or facts which constitute conditions precedent to acts by the Trustee or are in any other manner germane to the affairs of the Trust.

     D.   The Trustee may incorporate in one instrument those provisions of the original Declaration that remain unchanged, adding thereto all changes by amendments and deleting all provisions removed by amendments or otherwise and upon the execution and the recording by the Trustee thereof, same shall constitute the existing Declaration and Trust and any person, individual or corporation transacting business or dealing with the Trustee hereunder may accept a duplicate copy of the said existing Declaration of Trust acknowledged or certified by the Trustee as hereinafter provided as conclusive evidence of the present status of the Trust and a true copy thereof.

ARTICLE XXIII.

CAPTIONS

     The captions to the various Articles are used only as a matter of convenience and are not to be considered a part of said Articles or of this Declaration or to be used in determining the intent of the parties to it.

ARTICLE XXIV.

ILLEGALITY

     If any provision hereof be deemed illegal by final decision of a court of competent jurisdiction, the remainder of the Declaration shall nonetheless remain in full force and effect.

ARTICLE XXV.

MASSACHUSETTS TRUST

     The Trust shall be deemed to be a Massachusetts Trust and shall in all matters be governed by and interpreted in accordance with the laws of the Commonwealth of Massachusetts.

ARTICLE XXVI.

GENERAL

     The terms "Trustee" or "Trustees" when used in this instrument shall include both the singular and the plural where the context so permits and shall mean the Trustees from time to time in office and the Trustees executing this instrument; pronouns in the masculine shall include that feminine and the neuter where the context so permits. All documents executed pursuant hereto shall require the signature of all the Trustees then in office.

IN WITNESS WHEREOF, the said
set his/her/their hand(s) and seal(s) to this and to as many other counterparts as appropriate (each being in original) this   day of   , 19   .

_____   _____

Witness to signature(s)

_____

S.S   , 19

     Then personally appeared the above-named
                            acknowledge the foregoing instrument to be his/her/their free act and deed, before me,

_____

Notary Public:
    My commission expires:

Partnerships and Corporations

8

No book on asset protection would be complete without a discussion of partnerships and corporations and the important role each can play in the design of your financial fortress.

Most people connect partnerships and corporations with the protection of business interests and although it is true that these entities are frequently used for the conduct of business they can also be used to insulate personal or family assets, including a family home.

The Role of Partnerships in Asset Protection

Holding assets in a "partnership" form of organization can under certain circumstances provide excellent protection from creditors.

There are two major kinds of partnerships (1) general partnerships, and (2) limited partnerships. General partnerships serve no purpose as an asset protector and, in fact, can easily create many more liabilities than they can protect against. The limited partnership on the other hand, can often be a useful device for insulating assets.

How A Limited Partnership Works

The Uniform Limited Partnership Act defines a limited partnership as a partnership formed by two or more persons under the laws of a state and having one or more general partners and one or more limited or special partners. Limited partners are not bound by the obligations of the partnership provided they play no active role in the management of the partnership.

The Revised Uniform Limited Partnership Act defines person as a natural person, partnership, limited partnership (domestic or foreign), trust, estate, association or corporation.

It is not difficult to organize a limited partnership. A limited partnership is formed simply by filing Articles of Partnership in conformity with state laws.

A limited partnership consists of both general partners and limited partners. A general partner has rights, powers and obligations similar to those of partners in a general partnership, while a limited partner is one who only contributes capital primarily as a financial investment, with liability limited to loss of investment.

Since a general partner in a limited partnership has rights and powers comparable to those in a general partnership, he or she may become individually liable for all the debts of the firm. The general partner is also accountable to other partners as a fiduciary for any wrongdoings in the management of the partnership.

The rights of a limited partner are generally confined to the rights to have full accountings, basic information on business affairs and to receive a share of the income, and the same rights as a general partner in the dissolution and winding up of the partnership.

As noted earlier, a limited partner is liable for any losses of the partnership only to the extent of the partner's investment in the assets of the business. A limited partner is not liable as a general partner unless, in addition to the exercise of the limited partner's rights and powers as a limited partner, the partner also takes part in the control or management of the business. For example, a limited partner who permits the use of his name in the name of the limited partnership (except where the name is also the name of a general partner or the corporate name of the corporate general partner), is liable to creditors who extend credit to the limited partnership without actual knowledge that the limited partner is not a general partner. Otherwise, a limited partner is not liable for the obligations of the partnership unless the limited partner takes part in the control of the business. To this extent, the liability of a limited partner is similar to that of a stockholder in a corporation.

Rights of Creditors to a Partnership Interest

Armed with this information you are ready for the big question . . . How does a judgment creditor satisfy the individual debt by reaching the interest of a partner?

In practical terms the creditor pursuing a debtor whose only asset consists of an undivided interest in a limited partnership has to look to his share of the partnership proceeds after the partnership has been dissolved, the business affairs wound up, debts of the partnership satisfied and the share of the debtor-partner's surplus of the firm distributed. Alternatively, the creditor can look to attach the debtor's profits from the partnership. Each of these remedies may, however, be less than satisfying because: The partnership may not be soon dissolved and, in fact, dissolution may occur after the creditors judgment has expired. It is important to remember that the partners alone decide when a partnership shall terminate and this is a decision that cannot be enforced by a creditor of any one partner. Even when the partnership is dissolved, there may be nothing left for a partner (or his creditors) once partnership debts are paid. Nor can a creditor confidently anticipate profits, as profits may not be payable from the partnership but may instead be paid in the form of salaries (possibly as salaries to other family members as general partners) resulting in no surplus from which to pay profits.

This does not mean a limited partner's creditors are completely powerless.

The Uniform Limited Partnership Act provides that a judgment creditor (or, in some jurisdictions, any creditor) of a limited partner can obtain a court order charging a limited partner's interest in the partnership with payment of any unsatisfied amount of a judgment debt. The statute also provides that such interest may be redeemed with the separate property of any general partner, but may not be redeemed with partnership property.

The charging order is intended to protect partners of a partnership that have nothing to do with the claims of creditors of the individual partner. A judgment creditor of a partner may obtain a charging order by making due application to a court which then charges the interest of the debtor partner with payment of the unsatisfied amount of the judgment. The court may then or later appoint a receiver of the partner's share of the profits, and of any other money due or to be due him from the partnership.

Section 22 of The Uniform Limited Partnership Act provides that:

"(1) On due application to a court of competent jurisdiction by any judgment creditor of a limited partner, the court may charge the interest of the indebted limited partner with payment of the unsatisfied amount of the judgment debt; and may appoint a receiver, and make all other orders, directions, and inquiries which the circumstances of the case may require.

(2) The interest may be redeemed with the separate property of any general partner, but may not be redeemed with partnership property.

(3) The remedies conferred by paragraph (1) shall not be deemed exclusive of others which may exist.

(4) Nothing in this act shall be held to deprive a limited partner of his statutory exemption."

Where The Uniform Limited Partnership Act has been adopted, the charging order is the exclusive remedy of the judgment creditor in respect to the partner's interest in the firm. Where the judgment debtor fails to object to its entry, the co-partners, have no standing to oppose it.

The Uniform Partnership Act suggests two methods whereby the interest charged may be redeemed by the partnership at any time before foreclosure or of a sale directed by the court. First, any one or more of the partners may redeem or purchase the debtor-partner's interest with their separate property. The alternative method is for any one or more of the partners, with the consent of all the partners whose interests are not so charged or sold, to redeem or purchase the debtor-partner's interest with partnership property.

Still, even after foreclosure and sale, the creditor may be far from collecting on his debt. At the foreclosure sale, only the partner's interest, not specific assets of the partnership, is sold. It is unlikely that a limited partnership interest will bring a high price from third parties because of the limited role to which the purchaser is relegated. If the creditor becomes the purchaser, the creditor will still be entitled to only receive the charged partner's profits. Moreover, until dissolution occurs, the creditor (or his buyer) has no right to an accounting or rights to a surplus.

The principal change in the creditor's current status as a result of the foreclosure and sale is that the creditor now owns the partner's entire financial interest in the partnership, including all amounts ultimately due the partner on dissolution after settlement of liabilities. After the charge and the entry of payment and other orders, the debtor continues to be a partner in all respects except distributions and withdrawals from the firm. Moreover, the charging creditor is not even in the position as an assignee of the debtor's interest, but is burdened with an even less valuable interest.

The non-debtor partners have several options in dealing with the threat to the continuity of the partnership posed by a charged interest. They may forestall the threat of foreclosure by redeeming the charged interest before foreclosure with their own property or, if they all consent, with partnership property.

Should the partners redeem the interest for the amount of the debt, and if this is less than the value fixed by the court, the court may treat this as a loan to the debtor-partner, or order that the redeeming partners hold the interest in trust for the debtor-partner. If the court decrees foreclosure, the non-debtor-partners may buy the interest at the foreclosure sale.

Conversely, the non-debtor-partner, either before or after foreclosure, can remove the uncertainty created by the creditor's presence by dissolving the firm and buying the assets on liquidation, however, the partners must account on dissolution to the charging creditor for the debtor-partner's interest.

In summary, the creditor seeking to go

after a limited partnership interest has a number of obstacles to overcome:

1. Take judgment against the debtor;

2. Prove that the debtor has an interest in the partnership firm;

3. Obtain a charging order from a court;

4. Obtain appointment of a receiver to receive distributions of earnings or surplus upon liquidation;

5. Apply for foreclosure on the debtor-partner's partnership interest;

6. Pursue a forced sale of partner's interest at the foreclosure; (If the creditor is the purchaser, he can only receive the charged partner's cash flow; no right to accounting;)

7. Obtain judicial dissolution of the partnership;

8. Upon dissolution, obtain whatever share would have come to the debtor-partner after payment of all partnership creditors and claims of co-partners.

From a debtor's point of view, a limited partnership shields a debtor-partner's interest from the reach of all but the most-determined creditors. A creditor has to cross many hurdles before realizing any satisfaction on his debt. More often than not, a creditor may hold nothing more than a charging order against the interest of the limited partner which can generally be settled and discharged for a nominal sum considering the negligible value of the partnership interest in the hands of the creditor.

Two Ways A Corporation Can Protect You

Corporations are an essential weapon in any asset protection arsenal because a corporation can both:

• protect you from liability

• shield assets from creditor claims

A corporation is a distinct, legal entity separate and apart from its members, stockholders, directors or officers. Although it is a separate entity, it can act only through its members, officers or agents. A stockholder is not the employer of those working for the corporation nor is he the owner of corporate property. More importantly, a stockholder generally has no obligations for corporate obligations.

A corporation is a citizen of the state wherein it is created. A corporation does not cease to be a citizen of the state in which it is incorporated by engaging in business or acquiring property in another state. Since corporations are solely creatures of statute, the powers of a corporation in another state are derived from the constitution and laws of the state in which it is incorporated.

The existence of the corporation is not affected by the death or bankruptcy of a shareholder or by the transfer of his shares, and therefore has a continuous existence and is immortal as long as it complies with the annual requirements of the state in which it is incorporated.

Using Corporations to Avoid Liability

There is one important reason why you should be incorporated, plus many miscellaneous advantages and benefits to be gained. Foremost, of course, is the limited liability or protection of your personal assets from the creditors of the corporation should the corporation be unable to satisfy its obligations.

Once you create a corporation you have created an independent legal entity. The creditors of a corporation can proceed only against the assets of the corporation to satisfy corporate obligations. Corporate creditors cannot ordinarily proceed against the stockholders or officers, directors or other agents and employees.

There are several important exceptions to this rule which should be observed:

1.   Parties who guaranty corporate obligations can, of course, be held personally liable on their guaranty.

2.   Employees who are negligent or commit other wrongful acts can, together with the corporation, be held personally liable.

3.   Corporate officers and other responsible parties can be liable for unpaid withholding taxes and similar (sale, meals, etc.) taxes.

4.   Corporate directors can be personally liable for a number of fiduciary violations arising from their duties as directors.

Tip

If you are a corporate director, read **How To Avoid Liability As A Corporate Director** *(available from Enterprise Publishing, Inc.). It pinpoints a number of common causes of director liability and the safeguards you can take.*

Aside from these relatively rare incidents, where you can have personal exposure, most debts that arise from the operation of a business impose no personal liability. It goes without saying then that almost every professional or businessman needs a corporation simply because of the limited liability advantages associated with a corporation. Some ask, "does it make any difference whether I use a C corporation or an S corporation?" Remember the C is the standard corporation whereas the S is a small corporation taxed like a partnership or proprietorship where the corporation itself pays no taxes. There is no difference between the S and the C as to liability protection. Either can assure good liability protection if you remember to look and act at all times like a corporation.

Even if you are the corporation's sole employee you should incorporate for the liability protection it affords. Accountants do not always agree with this advice, but accountants consider incorporating from a strict taxation viewpoint and do not always consider liability issues. Considering S corporations present the same tax features as an unincorporated business, it is difficult to imagine why anyone would choose to bypass the protection of a corporation when business ventures always pose so much risk.

Many individuals argue "Well, I am the key person in the business" or "I am the licensed professional in the corporation so I have the liability exposure anyway." Realize that there are many lawsuits that do arise, however, for which the liability exposure would not have extended to you if you had been incorporated. Rather, it would have gone to the corporation.

Look at incorporation as the best personal asset protection insurance you can buy—it can protect your assets from staggering liabilities should your business fail.

Tip

Incorporation need not be expensive. See **How To Form Your Own Corporation Without a Lawyer for Under $50**, *published by Enterprise Publishing, Inc.*

Corporations are particularly recommended for anyone involved in hazardous activities such as contractors, trucking firms, etc. In addition, use corporations when involved in joint ventures with other individuals in which you might be held jointly or severally liable under failure of the joint venture. This is suggested because courts unanimously hold that when a joint venture is found to exist, partnership principles govern. Each of the joint venturers will be held liable as general partners should anything go wrong or any injury occur on the premises of the business several years later, for example. As general partners, the joint venturers will be liable to the extent of their personal assets should the assets of the joint venture be insufficient to satisfy the liability. For these reasons, doing business as a corporation will greatly reduce the likelihood of liability.

Tip

General partners in a limited partnership commonly select the corporate form of organization for purposes of eliminating the personal liability of its principals.

If you have several business activities you should also consider the multiple corporation approach. There are many corporations who find it to their advantage to use two or more corporations. For example, if you have two retail stores, each should be separately incorporated. Should one fail, its failure would have no effect on the other. You may also want to set up separate corporations when one activity is more risky or liability prone than another.

Lumberyards, for example, often set up a corporation for the retail and wholesale store but with a separate corporation for the manufacturing of trusses which could create awesome liability should the trusses collapse a home. This principle can be applied to many other businesses.

Tip

Always hold the more valuable

assets in the less vulnerable corporation. Corporations with high exposure should hold few assets. Because the risk-prone corporation has few assets in jeopardy you may be able to eliminate costly insurance coverage.

Courts have routinely upheld the strategy of using separate corporations to minimize or dilute liability. But to be treated as separate corporations for liability purposes the corporations must act separately. This means there can be no commingling of funds, or assets and liabilities as between corporations. It is also good practice to have different directors and separate corporate meetings. Properly maintained corporate records is an absolute must.

Tip

For a convenient way to maintain proper corporate records order **The Complete Book of Corporate Forms** *(Enterprise Publishing, Inc.).*

Corporations as an Asset Protection Tool

Corporations can also be an ideal way to hold personal assets such as a home, stocks and bonds or motor vehicles. Assuming the transfer of assets to the corporation was not in fraud of creditors, personal creditors will be unable to attach these assets as they are properly under corporate ownership.

Of course, there must be some consideration paid by the corporation in return for the transfer of assets. This consideration can be in the form of capital or equity (shares of stock in the corporation) or as debt (loans or notes due from the corporation).

Assuming you transfer your home to a corporation and receive in exchange either stock in the corporation or promissory notes (or both), your creditors could reach these shares or notes as they are your personal

assets.

However, it is frequently easier to protect corporate shares or notes than it is to shield tangible assets such as a home. In the first place, unlike real estate, there is no public record listing the stockholders of a privately-held corporation. Then too, it is relatively easy to transfer the corporate shares (or notes) as security for possible loans you owe family members. Alternatively, the shares or notes can be transferred to a trust, limited partnership or even another corporation. In effect, it can become extremely difficult for personal creditors to reach your interest in a corporation and thus a corporation can be considered as an alternative to a trust or limited partnership as a vehicle to hold assets, although there are tax and other factors that may give one preference over another.

When using a corporation to hold family assets, the key is to place ownership of the stock with a spouse (or separate entity) who is not vulnerable to creditors. It is not necessary for the stockholder to be active in the managerial affairs of the corporation and, in fact, the stockholder need not be an officer, director or employee. What is important is that the stockholder exercise all stockholders rights to prove the shareholder is not merely holding the stock as a "straw" for the debtor.

For this reason, the stockholder must be prepared to show that he or she:

1. Paid the consideration (subscription price) for the issuance of shares to the stockholder, and

2. Duly voted on all stockholder matters at general or special meetings of the stockholders.

Because corporate tax returns require disclosure of the stockholders in closely-held corporations, creditors commonly ask for copies of the tax returns. Make certain the tax records coincide with other disclosures concerning corporate ownership or your claims of ownership will lose credibility and weaken any attempts to place the corporate stock beyond the reach of creditors.

LIMITED PARTNERSHIP AGREEMENT

Agreement made on this, the   day of   19   , by and between   , having a business address of   (herein the "General Partner") and   , having a business address of   (hereinafter the "Limited Partner").

WHEREAS, the parties hereto are desirous of forming a Limited Partnership for those purposes which are hereinafter more particularly described; and

WHEREAS, the parties hereto are desirous of establishing the policies, procedures and methods of operation of the Limited Partnership as well as their respected rights, duties and obligations;

NOW, THEREFORE, in consideration of the mutual covenants herein contained and good and valuable consideration exchanged by and between the parties, receipt of which is hereby acknowledged, the parties do hereby agree, covenant and contract as follows:

ARTICLE I.

FORMATION OF LIMITED PARTNERSHIP

1.   The parties do hereby associate and form a domestic limited partnership pursuant to the provisions of   the Uniform Limited Partnership Act (the "Act").

2.   The parties do hereby agree to provide all data and information necessary for or incidental to the preparation of a Certificate of Limited Partnership, as provided for by the Act, and to thereafter execute such Certificate in duplicate and file the same with the office of the   , all as required by the Act. The General Partner shall, upon receipt of a Certificate from the office of the Secretary of State marked "Filed", promptly deliver or mail a copy of said Certificate of Limited Partnership to the Limited Partner.

196

ARTICLE II.

NAME, PURPOSE, PRINCIPAL OFFICE, TERM

1.   The business of the limited partnership shall be conducted under the name
of   (herein referred to as
the "Partnership").

2.   The business of the Partnership shall be

3.   The principal place of business of the Partnership shall be

4.   The term of the Partnership shall be twenty (20) years commencing on the
date of execution hereof, as above set forth and terminating at midnight on the day before
twenty (20) years next following the date hereof, unless sooner terminated as hereinafter
provided.

ARTICLE III.

BUSINESS CAPITAL

1.   shall be the General Partner of the
Partnership.

2.   shall be the Limited Partner of the
Partnership. The contribution of the Limited Partner to the Partnership is

ARTICLE IV.

PROFITS AND LOSSES

1.   All profits and losses derived or recognized from the operation of the
business of the Partnership shall be allocated as follows: to the General Partner, fifty
(50%) percent thereof; and, to the Limited Partner, fifty (50%) percent thereof.

2.   All allocations concerning profit and loss and all determinations regarding
the time and manner in which any expenses or obligations of the Partnership are
amortized or repaid, shall be made in the sole discretion of the General Partner.

3.   There shall be established and maintained for each partner a Capital
Account and an Income Account. Each partner's capital contribution and distributive
share of cash, profit and losses shall be reflected on their respective Capital or Income
Account as the case may be.

4.   No Limited Partner shall be personally liable for the debts, liabilities or financial obligations of the Partnership in excess of the amount contributed by the Limited Partner to the capital of the Partnership.

5.   The fiscal year end of the Partnership shall be December 31st.

ARTICLE V.

SALE OF PARTNERSHIP ASSETS

Should the real property held by the Partnership be at any time sold, the net profit realized from such sale shall be allocated in such proportion as is provided for in Article IV, Section 1.

ARTICLE VI.

MANAGEMENT, DUTIES, RESPONSIBILITIES

1.   <u>General Partner</u>

   a)   The General Partner shall manage the business and affairs of the Partnership and shall devote such time thereto as is necessary to properly accomplish the same. The General Partner is under no obligation to devote his full time to the business of the Partnership and may engage independently in the ownership, operation or management of other real estate projects or businesses. The General Partner is authorized by and on behalf of the Partnership, as evidenced by the execution hereof by all Partners, to borrow or lend money to make, deliver or accept any commercial paper; to execute and deliver any and all documents or instruments necessary for or incidental to the business of the Partnership, including without limitation, offers, contracts, deeds, leases, mortgages, bonds and the like and to otherwise deal with and contract to sell or sell any property of the Partnership, and, to agree or contract with any other person, firm or entity for the performance of services or the providing of goods and materials relative to the business of the Partnership notwithstanding any relationship or interest the General Partner may have with such person, firm or entity; provided always, that all things done by or at the direction of the General Partner be in the best interest of the purposes of the Partnership.

   b)   The General Partner of the Partnership shall be subject to liability to the same extent as if a partner in partnership without limited partners.

c) The General Partner shall not sell, assign, transfer, pledge or hypothecate, nor mortgage his interest in or otherwise enter into any agreement as the result of which any person, firm or entity shall become interested in the Partnership without the consent of the Limited Partner being first obtained which consent may be upon such terms, provisions and conditions as the Limited Partner may determine.

2. Limited Partner

a) No Limited Partner shall participate in the management of the business and affairs of the Partnership. Except in the case of distribution of assets upon liquidation, no Limited Partner shall have the right to demand or receive property other than case in return for his contribution to the capital of the Partnership.

b) No additional Limited Partners shall be admitted to the Partnership.

c) The Limited Partner shall not sell, assign, transfer, pledge or hypothecate, nor mortgage his interest in or otherwise enter into any agreement as the result of which any person, firm or entity shall become interested in the Partnership without the consent of all remaining Partner(s) being first obtained, which consent may be upon such terms, provisions and conditions as said remaining Partner(s) may determine.

d) The Limited Partner hereby consents, as evidenced by his execution hereof, to any sale or other disposition, encumbrance, mortgage or lease by the General Partner, on behalf of the Partnership, of any or all of the Partnership's assets, now or hereafter acquired, on such terms, provisions and conditions as may be determined in the sole discretion of the General Partner and the engagement, when and if required, as determined in the sole discretion of the General Partner, of and to such brokers, agent and attorneys as are necessary for or incidental to the business of the Partnership, notwithstanding any relationship or interest the General Partner may have with such brokers, agents or attorneys.

ARTICLE VII.

COMPENSATION

No Partner shall receive any salary or compensation for services rendered to or on behalf of the Partnership in the capacity of a Partner, nor shall any Partner receive any interest on his contribution to the capital of the Partnership.

ARTICLE VIII.

DEATH, RETIREMENT, INCAPACITY OR INSOLVENCY OF PARTNER

1.   The death or incapacity of a Limited Partner shall not dissolve or terminate the business of the Partnership. Notwithstanding any provision hereof to the contrary, the interest of a Limited Partner in the Partnership may be transferred by testamentary disposition or upon intestate succession in accordance with the laws of

pertaining to descent and distribution; provided, that any person or persons succeeding to the interest of a Limited Partner, as provided for within Section VIII, shall not entitle such successor or successors to exercise any rights as a Limited Partner but shall entitle such successor or successors to receive such distributions as the deceased Limited Partner would have been entitled to receive in accordance with the provisions hereof.

2.   Upon the death, retirement or incapacity of the General Partner or in the event the General Partner (i) makes an assignment for the benefit of creditors; (ii) files a voluntary petition in bankruptcy; (iii) is adjudicated a bankrupt or insolvent; (iv) files a petition or answer seeking for himself any reorganization, arrangement, composition or readjustment of his debts and obligations or other court pleading admitting or failing to contest the material allegations of a petition filed against him in any proceeding of such nature or (v) seeks or consents to, or acquiesces in the appointment of a trustee or receiver for the liquidation of all or substantially all his assets, then and in such event, the Partnership shall be expeditiously terminated following the winding up of the business of the Partnership and the distribution of its assets.

3.   In the event of the death or incapacity of the general Partner, the business of the Partnership shall be wound up and the Partnership terminated by the legal representative or representatives of the General Partner.

ARTICLE IX.

TERMINATION AND LIQUIDATION OF THE PARTNERSHIP

1.   The business of the Partnership may be terminated by the General Partner at any time prior to the expiration of its term, upon not less than ninety (90) days prior written notice by the General Partner to the Limited Partner. In such event or upon the occurrence of any event enumerated in Paragraph 2 of Section VIII, the General Partner or his legal representative shall wind up and liquidate the Partnership in either of the following manners:

a) By selling the assets of the Partnership and after the payment of all Partnership liabilities and obligations, by distributing the net proceeds therefrom to the Partners in such proportions as provided for in Article V hereof; or

b) By distribution of the assets of the Partnership in kind, each Partner accepting an undivided interest in the Partnership assets, subject to its liabilities, in which event each Partner shall receive an undivided interest in such property equal to the portion of the proceeds to which he would have been entitled as provided for in Article V hereof if such property were sold.

Upon liquidation in either of the foregoing manners, the Partnership shall be deemed terminated whereupon any and all documents necessary or incidental to evidencing such termination shall be prepared and filed with the office of the

2. The General Partner shall not be personally liable to the Limited Partner for a deficit or deficiency in the Limited Partner Capital Account or for the return of their contribution to the capital of the Partnership.

3. In the event of a liquidating distribution of Partnership property in kind, the fair market value of such property shall be determined by an appraiser mutually agreed upon by the Partners.

ARTICLE X.

POWER OF ATTORNEY

The Limited Partner hereto constitutes and appoints the General Partner his true and lawful attorney to make, execute, sign, acknowledge, and file a Certificate of Limited Partnership or amendments thereto, and upon termination of the Partnership, a Certificate of Dissolution, as required under the laws of the
and to include therein all information required by the laws of the Commonwealth of Massachusetts, and also to make, execute, sign, acknowledge, deliver and file such other instruments as may be required under the laws of the
The General Partner is authorized to take title to the real property herein referred to and to execute any and all documents related thereto on behalf of the Partnership, whether or not a Certificate of Limited Partnership has been filed prior to the date of such acceptance of title or execution of such documents, and all of the parties hereto hereby ratify and confirm any such action by the General Partner.

ARTICLE XI.

BANKING

All funds of the Partnership shall be deposited in its name in such checking account or accounts as shall be designated by the General Partner. All withdrawals therefrom are to be made upon checks signed by the General Partner or his legal representative acting on behalf of the General Partner as provided for herein.

ARTICLE XII.

CONVEYANCE

Any deed, bill of sale, mortgage, security agreement, lease, contract of sale or other commitment purporting to convey or encumber the interest of the Partnership in all or any portion of any real or personal property at any time held in its name, shall be signed by the General Partner as provided for herein and no other signature shall be required.

ARTICLE XIII.

BOOKS

The Partnership shall maintain full and complete books and records at its principal office, or such office as shall be designated for such purpose by the General Partner, and all Partners shall have the right to inspect and examine books at all reasonable times. The books shall be closed and balanced at the end of each fiscal year.

ARTICLE XIV.

ARBITRATION

In the event a dispute shall arise between the Partners which the Partners are unable to resolve, prior, and as a condition precedent to, the commencement of legal proceedings seeking the dissolution of the Partnership, such dispute shall be submitted to the Regional Office of the American Arbitration Associates, for arbitration before a single arbitrator in accordance with the Rules and Procedures of the Association. The prevailing party shall be entitled to receive and recover from the non-prevailing party or parties, all costs, fees and expenses, including reasonable attorneys fees, incurred in the prosecution or defense as the case may be of such arbitration.

ARTICLE XV.

<u>INDEMNITY</u>

The Partnership shall indemnify and save harmless the General Partner, out of the assets of the Partnership, from any personal loss, damage, cost or expense incurred by him by reason of any act performed by him in good faith and on behalf of the Partnership and in furtherance of its interests or in the defense of any claim, suit or action in which they may be involved by reason of his serving as General Partner hereunder excluding only actions arising out of gross negligence, willful misconduct or in connection with matters in which the General Partner may have not acted in a reasonable belief that his action was lawful and in the best interest of the Partnership.

ARTICLE XVI.

<u>NOTICES</u>

All notices provided for in this agreement shall be directed to the parties at the address hereinabove set forth and to the Partnership at its principal office by registered or certified mail, postage prepaid, return receipt requested.

The within Limited Partnership Agreement, executed in duplicate original copies is to take effect as a sealed instrument, is to be construed in accordance with the laws of

and is binding upon the parties hereto their respective, heirs, executors, administrators, successors and assigns.

IN WITNESS WHEREOF, the parties hereunto set their hands and seals on the day and date first above-written.

_____	_____
Witness to signature(s)	General Partner

_____
Limited Partner

Answers to Common Questions

9

Q. Can one IRS levy on my paycheck allow the IRS to take subsequent paychecks or are separate levies required to attach each paycheck?

A. The Tax Reform Act of 1976 made several important changes in IRS power to seize wages and salaries. In the past the IRS was allowed to keep the entire paycheck and the taxpayer got nothing. But the IRS always had to come back with another Notice of Levy to seize additional paychecks. Under the present code provisions you will be able to keep a part of your paycheck, even if it is just barely enough to buy groceries. The IRS paycheck seizure now works just like a garnishment and the seizure remains in effect, either until it is released or the taxes are paid in full. This means that unless you take immediate action to fully pay your taxes or attempt to work something out at the local IRS office, your boss will have to give the IRS a large chunk of every paycheck.

Q. What percentage of my paycheck can I keep under an IRS levy?

A. The code allows certain exemptions from IRS seizures on wages, salaries, or other income. You will be allowed $75 per week for yourself and $25 per week for your spouse and an additional $25 per week for each dependent. For example, if you normally clear $250 per week and have a wife and three children, you will be able to retain $175 ($75 for yourself and $25 for your wife, plus $75 for a total of 3 children), and the IRS gets the balance of $75 ($250 less $175 = $75).

Q. What personal assets, if any, are exempt from IRS seizure?

A. Wearing apparel, schoolbooks, furniture and personal effects (up to $1,500 value), tools of a trade or profession, unemployment benefits, certain annuity and pension payments, workmen's compensation, and child support payments.

Q. Can the IRS seize IRA and unqualified pension plans?

A. Generally IRA and other unqualified pension funds are subject to IRS seizure just as they can be reached by other creditors.

Q. What can be done to avoid an IRS levy of bank accounts?

A. Short of reaching settlement with the IRS, the most practical strategy is to remove excess funds from all bank and checking accounts in advance of the levy. Many taxpayers open accounts with new banks and thus stay one step ahead of the IRS. Others prefer to keep their funds in a spouse's account or issue checks from corporations or other entities they may own.

Q. What can be done when the IRS seizes property in which there is little or no equity?

A. IRS policy prohibits Revenue Officers from seizing property when the equity in the property is insufficient "to yield net proceeds from sale to apply to the unpaid tax liabilities" (IRM 5341.21:[1]). Furthermore, any officer who seizes such property must release it immediately (IRM 5341.21:[5]). If it is determined that there is sufficient equity in the seized property to pay for the expenses of sale, but the net proceeds from the sale will be small in comparison to the tax liability, the officer and his group manager must decide if pursuing the seizure and sale is warranted (IRM 5342.21:[6]).

If the IRS has seized your property and your equity in the property is either insufficient to pay for the expenses of seizure and sale or small in comparison to the tax liability, you should demand that the seizure be released under the provisions of IRM 5341.22.

Q. How does the IRS determine the minimum "bid" price for seized assets?

A. Before a sale the officer must establish a "minimum bid price" for the property—the lowest price at which the officer will sell the property. If the property cannot be sold at that price, the IRS will "buy-in" or purchase the property for the U.S. Government at the minimum bid price and credit your tax account for that amount.

The minimum bid price is computed by a formula that starts with a determination of the fair market value of the property. The fair market value is then reduced by 25 percent, and that figure multiplied by 80 percent or more to compute the forced-sale equity. The minimum bid price is then computed by subtracting the amount of any liens prior to the tax lien (for example, a first mortgage on a house) from the forced sale equity. And in no event can the minimum bid price exceed the total taxes, penalties, interest, and other charges on the account.

It is important that you protect yourself from an unreasonably low evaluation of the value of your seized property. You have the right to object to the minimum bid price and the right to object to how it was computed. You also have the right to request that an IRS valuation engineer, or a professional appraiser, assist in determining the property's true forced-sale value. Be aware, though, that the costs of obtaining a private appraisal will be charged back to you.

Q. How long can the IRS chase a taxpayer for delinquent taxes?

A. From the date the tax has been assessed, the IRS has six years within which to legally collect the delinquency. The day following the end of the sixth year the IRS has no legal authority to compel payment or enforce collection unless the statute of limitations has been extended in some manner. Revenue Officers are under strict instructions not to let the statutory period expire on an open case. Officers have been fired or demoted for allowing the statute to expire. When a statute has less than a year before expiring, an officer will attempt to obtain your signature on Form 900, "Tax Collection Waiver," to agree to extend the time period of the statute. If you do not sign the waiver and extend the statutory period, you may find yourself under considerable pressure from the IRS. Revenue Officers use every legal power they have to collect the tax before the statutory period expires. They may begin seizing anything and everything in sight, hardship or no hardship, to satisfy a tax claim before the statute of limitations expires.

Q. How does the IRS determine what assets a taxpayer owns?

A. The IRS will ask the taxpayer to voluntarily file a financial statement listing all assets. If the taxpayer fails to cooperate, the IRS has the power to summons the taxpayer (and his financial records) and to compel disclosure through court order and criminal sanctions. Of course, the IRS also relies on previously filed tax returns to uncover assets. It is unlawful to fraudulently conceal assets or to intentionally falsify information provided to the IRS.

Q. Can a taxpayer legally transfer his home after a tax liability is incurred but before a tax lien is filed?

A. The general rules applicable to fraudulent transfers extend to the IRS as well, however, transferring property to a different title can be an effective and legal means of preserving assets from an IRS tax lien. Many taxpayers adopt the practical attitude that they have little to lose by the attempted transfer whereas they are certain to lose if they do nothing and allow the IRS tax lien to attach. Surprisingly, the IRS has not been overly active in recovering conveyed property. This is one area where the guidance of experienced counsel is essential.

Q. Can property subject to an IRS lien be transferred?

A. The law does not prevent a person from selling his assets even if there are outstanding liens on the property. Under most state laws the liens would remain with the property after a transfer or sale has been made. The IRS will not even question the sale of property encumbered with tax liens unless it appears that the sale was for "less than good and valuable consideration." But a sale of encumbered property (that is, property secured by a tax lien) for less

than full market value could present problems. And a sale of encumbered property to a relative for less than full market value will raise even more problems.

Q. What remedies does the IRS have once it discovers a fraudulent conveyance of a taxpayers assets?

A. 1. The IRS may file suit in a U.S. District Court to have the transfer or sale set aside. This action reinstates the property to its original owner, the transferor, and makes it subject to seizure by the IRS. This procedure is generally the preferred remedy in federal tax cases when the IRS has a particular interest in that specific piece of property.

2. The IRS may file a suit to obtain a judgment against the transferee. A judgment can be requested for the value of the transferred property but not exceeding the amount owed by the delinquent taxpayer.

3. The IRS may begin an administrative civil proceeding to assess against the transferee an amount of money equal to the value of the transferred property but not exceeding the amount owed by the delinquent taxpayer. This proceeding follows the normal tax assessment route, thereby giving the transferee the right to appeal to the Tax Court. If assessed, the amount owed can be collected in the same manner as delinquent taxes.

Q. In terms of asset protection is it advisable for a married couple to file a joint return?

A. By filing a joint tax return you may be subjecting all of your assets to possible enforcement action of the IRS. Seizures of real estate are popular with Revenue Officers because they are relatively easy to do. The ideal collection situation involves married taxpayers who owe a lot of money, own real estate with a substantial equity, and who file a joint tax return. Filing a joint tax return makes it especially easy for the

IRS to collect when there is jointly owned real estate involved because officers know they have more leverage to encourage the taxpayer to borrow the money or raise it in some way as the IRS can seize and sell full title to the property.

Even though filing a separate return could mean an increased tax bill, it may be advisable to do so when you cannot possibly pay or borrow the money you would otherwise owe if you had filed a joint return. Filing a separate return may also be far easier than trying to transfer your assets from one form of ownership to another. If you have any questions about whether filing a separate return would be advisable in your situation, you should discuss it with your tax practitioner or attorney.

Q. What strategies can I use to protect family assets if either my spouse or I are forced to go on Medicaid?

A. There are many families who have been financially wiped out because one spouse requires extended nursing home care and therefore seeks benefits under state or federal Medicaid or welfare programs. There are two basic approaches used to qualify for Medicaid while preserving family assets.

1. *Revocable Trusts:* Under this approach the widow or widower who may at some future date have to go on welfare, transfers or gifts assets to family members. The children then establish a grantor trust known as a revocable living trust with the grantors themselves, i.e., the children, and the parent or parents, as beneficiaries of the trust. For tax purposes all income is generally taxable to the children, (the grantors who set up the trust). The income from such assets can be available for the use of a parent as beneficiary who later goes into a rest home or on certain welfare programs and yet not constitute a disqualification of benefits since the parent no longer owns the property.

2. *Irrevocable Trusts:* The use of the irrevocable trust for this purpose is also endorsed by many lawyers who now prefer this particular approach. They find the irrevocable trust a better option because it cannot be revoked, amended or altered and therefore, the interest of one who may require Medicaid is fixed by the terms of the trust document itself. Under this approach, someone generally other than mother or father creates an irrevocable trust. Mother or father may then gift assets over a period of perhaps years to the irrevocable trust in much the same manner as mother and dad could have gifted property directly to the children. When this strategy is used, mother or dad are not the trustees but become beneficiaries of the trust.

A similar approach involves assets gifted over a period of time to children or other family members who then, at a later point in time, themselves set up an irrevocable trust. The children also gift assets of their own into the irrevocable trust for the benefit of multiple beneficiaries including mother and father. Regardless of the type trust used, one important clause should be inserted:

> *Restrictions:* The trustee is prohibited from making payments as reimbursement to any governmental entity which may have incurred expenses for the benefit of any beneficiary, and the Trustees shall not pay any obligation of a beneficiary which obligation is or can otherwise be payable by any governmental entity or pursuant to any governmental program of reimbursement or payment.

It is important to make these transfers at least 24 months prior to any application for Medicaid assistance. The 24-month period to dispose of assets is to discourage disposing of assets by Medicaid applicants for less than fair market value for the sole purpose of qualifying for Medicaid assistance.

States are empowered to place liens against the estates of those receiving Medicaid benefits where it is discovered that assets have been transferred within 24 months prior to Medicaid application for less than fair market value.

Q. What happens if property subject to homestead is sold at auction sale for either more or less than the homestead amount?

A. If the homestead consists of only one piece of property, it cannot be sold should the bid not exceed the amount of the exemption. Only the value in excess of the homestead exemption will be subject to partition and sale. If the homestead is worth more than the allowed exemption, the debtor may elect to sell the homestead and receive the value of the homestead exemption and apply the balance to the judgment. The proceeds of the sale up to the amount of the exemption are paid to the debtor but are exempt from execution or attachment usually for periods of between six months and one year, depending upon state law.

Q. Is it possible to legally retain assets when bankruptcy is declared?

A. There are three possibilities which should be explored with counsel well in advance of the bankruptcy.

1. The use of a business trust, family limited partnership or corporation:

Assume the debtor puts $200,000 of assets into a business trust. Initially the husband has a 100% interest in this business trust but over several years gifts away his 100% interest to children, parents or other family members leaving himself holding no interest in the trust. The husband can continue during his bankruptcy to act as a trustee and manager of the trust with control over the assets of the trust even though, for insolvency purposes he owns a zero value in the business trust.

Bankruptcies would generally not cause the loss of the assets previously transferred to the business trust assuming it was done far enough in advance.

Family limited partnerships and corporations can be used to accomplish the same result.

2. Outright gifts:

Under federal gift tax exclusions, one may gift $10,000 in value per year to as many donees as desired. In addition, there is a unified credit available for each individual as of 1987 in the amount of $600,000. Therefore, one person can gift $610,000 on January 1, 1991, as an example. Many individuals enjoy a long record of gifting assets to family members, i.e., children, grandchildren, parents, etc. Some gift the assets outright. Others gift the assets to family members who later transfer the gifted asset to family limited partnerships effectively under the control of the grantor. If done correctly, these gifts, undertaken for estate planning or income tax reasons, are generally safe under a future bankruptcy. Frequently, gifted assets at a later point can perhaps be loaned back to mother and dad to get them established in a business, or to buy a new home. Children who have been the recipients of the gifts may also, for example, set up a family business to employ the bankrupt parents. There are, of course, many variations of this concept.

3. Use homesteads and exemptions:

A third strategy is to redeploy non-exempt assets into exempt assets. For example, in Florida, a primary residence is fully protected under bankruptcy regardless of its value. There is nothing fraudulent, for example, in selling non-exempt assets (automobiles, stocks, etc.) prior to the bankruptcy and investing the funds either to buy a home subject to homestead or perhaps reducing the mortgage on the home. The objective is to file bankruptcy only with the protected home as an asset.

Q. Why would it not be preferable to hold title to a family home in the name of the less vulnerable spouse rather than in a limited partnership, trust or some other entity?

A. There are three important reasons. First, entrusting assets to a spouse may offer little protection in the event of a subsequent divorce. Second, although your spouse may appear less vulnerable, you cannot always be certain the less vulnerable spouse will remain immune from personal exposure. Lastly, it may be easier for creditors to set aside a transfer to a spouse than one made to a trust or partnership.

Q. To what extent can mortgages against property be an effective shield for property?

A. Placing valid mortgages against the property obviously offers excellent protection because there is then less equity for creditors to reach. A debtor may, for example, owe family members for prior loans which loans may be secured by mortgages against real estate, or as an encumbrance against automobiles, boats, etc.

A debtor may even borrow as much as possible from a bank or other lender to dissipate equity in the property. The proceeds may be used as "gifts" to family members or to repay family loans or possibly to invest into exempt or homesteaded property. More than one debtor has reported the loan proceeds have been gambled away. While truthful disclosure is strongly suggested, the important point is that cash proceeds are difficult to trace or attach.

Q. Is it possible for business assets to be protected from creditors by having the owners loan money to their corporation and taking a mortgage in return?

A. It's not only possible, but an exceptionally wise practice.

Assume you find a business that re-

quires a $50,000 down payment. You pay the $50,000 into your newly formed corporation in return for all the shares of stock. On that basis, your entire investment is characterized as "equity" or "capital contribution."

Two years go by and your business becomes insolvent with $100,000 in debts. At auction, the assets bring $50,000. The creditors get the $50,000 at the rate of 50 cents on the dollar, and you as the stockholder receive nothing. Your plight becomes obvious; you not only lost your business, you lost $50,000 besides.

However, you can protect your investment by lending your corporation most of the money and using much smaller amounts to buy the shares.

In the above example, you could have loaned $40,000 to a close friend or relative, who in turn could have loaned the $40,000 to your corporation in return for a mortgage on the business assets as security. Your relative would be obligated to repay your loan only as the corporation pays its debts to him. With your remaining $10,000, you could buy the outstanding shares of the corporation and still be its sole stockholder.

If the business turns sour, your mortgage-holding relative would be entitled to the first $40,000 of auction proceeds (or whatever the corporation owes him at that point) *before* other creditors receive a cent. Once your relative is repaid, he could repay his loan to you. The bottom line is that you will have recouped $40,000 of your $50,000 investment by whittling that investment down to $10,000.

Since bankruptcy courts may nullify a loan made by a stockholder and give "arms-length" creditors priority, I recommend using an intermediary to make the loan to the corporation rather than making a direct loan yourself. A relative's loan is safe as long as he can prove he actually loaned the money.

This is perfectly legal. Should the idea of putting your own economic interests ahead of your creditors shock your conscience, that's morality, not business. You may choose to follow your own conscience, but you should insure that you will at least have a choice.

Review this strategy with your lawyer and accountant, so they can execute the necessary paperwork.

Q. Aside from acting prudently, what steps can I take to protect myself from liability arising from serving as a director of a large corporation?

A. It is vital that you obtain from the corporation an indemnification agreement compensating you for any liability or suits which you may become involved in as a consequence of your action as an officer or director of the corporation. Many insurance companies provide such liability protection to boards of directors and officers, although the cost of such premiums is rising dramatically and is very burdensome to many corporations.

You should, however, go beyond the indemnification agreement and require a specific policy of liability insurance to cover you. Furthermore, you must anticipate that the corporation could itself end up in bankruptcy which may nullify the indemnification agreement. You will then look for your protection to the directors' liability coverage policy that the corporation acquired.

Q. What is meant by a children's trust?

A. In tax law there is a trust known as a 2503 "C" children's trust, which is named after the section of the Internal Revenue Code that sets out the parameters applicable to this particular kind of trust.

Properly and timely funded, property transferred to the children's trust will remain out of the reach of the grantor's creditors, as it would with either a business trust or family limited partnership.

Although the children's trust is sometimes used to protect assets, it does have the inherent disadvantage that the trust assets do belong to the children and must ultimately be distributed to the children although the children's trust may legitimately loan assets or cash to the parents or others. Based on this one limitation, other trusts or limited partnerships are preferable as an asset protection device.

Q. Although IRA accounts can be attached, are there pension funds specifically exempt from attachment?

A. At present, it is generally held that pension benefits are exempt from garnishment until the actual receipt of the funds by pensioners. Other exempt properties or annuities have been judicially or statutorily stated as being exempt from attachment. Exemptions under the Employee Retirement Income Security Act (ERISA) include the federal judiciary annuities, railroad employee annuities, civil service workers retirement annuities and pensions, military service survivors and retirement benefits, central intelligence agency annuity benefits and veteran benefits. The predominant view of ERISA pensions is that they cannot be garnished, although at least one court has issued a contrary opinion.

Retirement plan funds are very likely to be garnished or subjected to attachment where the funds have vested in their recipient pensioner, unless the funds are required for the support of the pensioner. Even then, several exceptions exist. Should the pensioner file in bankruptcy, the funds will most likely be included as part of the estate rather than exempt property unless, possibly, the funds are not yet vested in the recipient. Retirement plans may possibly be protected from attachment and garnishment by including a spend-thrift clause or a non-assignability clause in the pension plan.

IRA and Keough plans are very likely to be garnished and not exempt from a debtor's estate in bankruptcy, or from general judgment creditors, especially where such funds are not considered to be essential for the support and maintenance of the recipient and/or where such funds are considered to be vested in the recipient.

Q. Are there ways a debtor can protect new assets from past judgments?

A. Probably the best way would be to acquire and hold the assets in a corporation in which the spouse and children (or other family members) would own all the stock in the new corporation. The husband, for example, could still be employed as chief officer of the corporation and serve on the board of directors without owning stock.

Future business accumulations by the corporation would be beyond the reaches of the past judgment creditors of the husband, inasmuch as he does not own anything in the new corporation. You can use either a "C" corporation or an "S" corporation since either type of corporation would provide adequate protection.

What is important is that the creditors must be unable to trace funds or property invested in the corporation to the debtor.

Limited partnerships and business trusts can be similarly used, however, a corporation is an easier entity to organize and deal with under these circumstances.

Q. In a risky business startup would it be a good idea to personally own the equipment and lease it to the business?

A. Assuming the business is incorporated, as it should be, leasing assets from its stockholders can make enormous sense. Should the business fail (as 80% do), the owners can simply reclaim the equipment rather than lose them to business creditors.

Real estate should never be owned by a small closely-held operating company. The real estate may be titled to a separate corporation, trust or limited partnership and leased to the operating company.

Similarly, valuable patents, trademarks, copyrights, licenses and distributorship agreements may benefit from ownership in an entity other than the more vulnerable operating company. Here the children's trust (IRC Sec. 2503 "C") ties in beautifully as an income tax saving device if the beneficiaries are age 14 or older. A frequent application is for the children's trust to own equipment and then lease the equipment to the family business (or family corporation). The assets held in trust are protected from lawsuits against the parents and the corporation.

Q. How can a principal in a family-owned corporation protect himself from liability on corporate guarantees?

A. Here's how you can limit your personal liability to the absolute minimum.

1. Never guarantee a debt unless you're certain the business can pay it off.

2. Banks and other institutional lenders never lend to small business without guarantees from the owners, so you can't avoid them if you want to get your hands on bank financing. But you can do it the right way. First, make certain the bank secures their note with a mortgage on the business assets. In the event the business fails, the bank is the first to get paid, decreasing your exposure on the note. Second, make certain the liquidation value of the assets is comparable to the balance owed the bank on the note. You don't want business assets yielding the bank only $30,000 if the note shows a balance of $50,000. They'll chase you for the remaining $20,000.

3. Just because one would-be creditor demands a guarantee doesn't mean they all will. A guarantee is a bargaining point when you seek out a new supplier. Shop around until you find suppliers who will extend credit to your corporation rather than you.

4. Make it firm policy never to guarantee an existing corporate debt. Why should you? You have nothing to gain. Let your account go into arrears and credit managers will plead, promise, threaten and cajole to get you to risk your personal assets to back up your now questionable account. Ignore their demands for a personal guarantee.

5. A guarantee is just one way to convince a creditor to extend credit to your corporation, but there are plenty of risk-saving alternatives. For example, you can offer a mortgage on the business assets. Whatever the collateral, confine your creditors' recourse to the corporation. Let the corporation exhaust its resources before you even consider a guarantee.

6. If you must supply your guarantee, negotiate it on a partial basis. Perhaps you have a key supplier to whom your business already owes $10,000. He refuses to extend further credit without a guarantee. If so, offer your guarantee to cover only the fresh credit. That way you won't be personally liable for the existing $10,000. Or limit the dollar amount on your guarantee.

7. Understand your creditor's position. Without your guarantee, he may decline shipment of a $20,000 order. But he may willingly gamble on a $10,000 order. Be prepared to cut orders to coincide with your company's credit rating.

8. If you have partners, make sure they also sign any guarantee. They enjoy the benefits of the business, so why not the risk? I can tell you one sad story of a 25% owner of a restaurant who guaranteed $86,000 in bills without "bothering" his other three partners. You guessed it. When the restaurant failed, his partners walked away, leaving him to satisfy the debt.

9. If your business shows signs of trouble, give priority to creditors holding your guarantee. Your objective is to pay them before your business collapses so they (and ultimately you) will incur no loss.

Q. Can a court compel one spouse to surrender his or her assets to satisfy the debts of the other spouse?

A. The courts universally maintain the separateness of property between husband and wife and do not allow creditors of one spouse to seize property of the other spouse in satisfaction of the other's debts. This is true even where the debtor spouse may have given the property to the non-debtor spouse, so long as it is not a violation of the fraudulent conveyances act.

Q. May a creditor compel a debtor to disclose assets in advance of a judgment?

A. Not generally. Discovery of assets is a post-judgment remedy which explains why many debtors protract litigation as long as possible — as it gives them ample time to dispose of assets. A creditor can use discovery to find out about assets if the claim includes allegations of fraudulent conveyance.

Q. May a creditor attach a debtor's home or assets prior to a judgment?

A. The answer depends on the nature of the claim. If the court believes the creditor is likely to win — as with an unpaid promissory note or other claim that is unspeculative, then the creditor may be granted a prejudgment attachment. More speculative or factual claims (negligence actions, for example) are not likely to win a prejudgment attachment nor are claims for which there is adequate insurance.

Q. If a husband transfers property to a wife in consideration for the wife's promise to furnish housekeeping and nursing care to him, will his promise constitute adequate consideration to defeat a fraudulent conveyance claim?

A. Probably not. First, executory agreements to be performed in the future generally are not sufficient to constitute adequacy of consideration under a fraudulent conveyance claim. Second, such an agreement violates public policy since spouses are considered to owe one another these duties by reason of their marital relationship.

Q. How valuable is a prenuptial agreement as an asset protection device?

A. Such agreements are enforceable provided the agreement does not contravene public policy or the laws of the particular state in which it is to be enforced. There are a number of practical uses for such an agreement:

1. Preserving the identity of separate property (i.e., property owned prior to marriage, or which is received by gift or inheritance, or is derived from the proceeds of the sale or exchange of separate property during the marriage);

2. Defining which assets accumulated during the marriage will be separate and which will be joint;

3. Insulating certain assets from family members or others (e.g., children from a previous marriage) who might otherwise have a claim to such property as beneficiaries of the grantor's estate;

4. Simplifying accounting to avoid tracing problems through the commingling of funds; and

5. Avoiding the estate plan which would otherwise be devised for the couple by the courts or the general operation of law.

Q. Can spouses in community property states determine between themselves whether their property shall be held as community property or separate property?

A. Agreements between husband and wife to convert separate property into community property or vice versa are common and generally accepted in law. Such agreements delineate property rights between the spouses. Statutory procedures are available for the transfer, or partition of community property. Agreements between husband and wife

may be made in contemplation of separation, or they may be made for tax purposes, or estate planning. Agreements between married persons that transfer or partition community property must contain the essential elements of a valid contract. Such agreements should, where appropriate, make provision for property that has not yet been acquired as well as existing property. When spouses wish to convert separate property into community property, a schedule of the spouse's separate property to be transferred should be included in the agreement.

Q. What type of fraudulent conveyance is easiest to set aside?

A. Gifts to family members are probably the easiest transfers to set aside. All a judgment creditor or a trustee in bankruptcy has to do is to ascertain the circumstances of the donor. Transfers to a spouse for "love and affection" are gifts, since they are not based on consideration. Thus, if such a transfer is made an intent to defraud can be inferred, particularly if it leaves the transferor insolvent in the face of a claim.

Q. What is meant by a spendthrift trust?

A. A spendthrift trust provides that the beneficiary's interest terminates upon an attempt to transfer or reach the interest, or upon bankruptcy of the beneficiary. The provision, if effective, merely prevents creditors from reaching the interest while still in trust. However, one cannot create a spendthrift trust for one's own benefit. Creditors can then reach the assets, but the trust is otherwise valid.

Q. Is conveyance into a trust subject to a gift tax?

A. A conveyance in trust is not subject to gift tax where the transferor retains control over the property transferred. Thus, if a transfer in trust is made to protect assets from creditors, and the transferor wants to avoid payment of gift tax, sufficient control over all or part of the assets transferred should be retained to avoid having the transfer deemed a completed gift.

Under Reg. 25.2511-2(b), a gift to a discretionary trust, where the trustee can distribute income and principal to the grantor with no reversion in the grantor, is normally a completed gift for gift tax purposes. However, under Rev.Rul. 76-103, if the grantor's creditors can reach the trust property under state law, no completed gift is made because the grantor is deemed to retain sufficient control.

Q. Can creditors of a legatee or beneficiary under a will attack the bequest?

A. Bequests and inheritances can generally be seized by creditors of the person receiving the bequest or inheritance at the time it is paid to him. Wills and trusts often have "spendthrift" provisions which protect a fiduciary or executor from having to pay the creditor of a person entitled to a portion of the trust or estate, but such provisions do not prevent the creditor from attaching or levying on the beneficiary's interest in a trust or estate once it has been paid over.

Bequests received within six months *after* filing for bankruptcy are also subject to seizure by the bankruptcy trustee.

Q. How long does a creditor have to enforce a judgment?

A. A judgment creditor has twenty years to obtain satisfaction of a judgment. It is therefore theoretically possible for a defendant to be brought into court for a supplementary reexamination process proceeding every year the judgment remains unsatisfied.

Q. How should automobiles be titled?

A. There is no particular rule for owning automobiles. The value of an automobile is not generally that significant in the totality of one's assets. There is one rule, however, which you should follow when considering who should take title to an automobile. Unless the automobile is being carried as an asset of a business, the person who is the primary driver of an automobile should be its owner. You do not want to create a situation where more than one person can be held legally responsible for an accident. For example, a wife negligently injures a pedestrian while driving a car owned by her husband, the victim can sue not only the wife, but also the husband on the theory that she is his agent. To the extent that husband and wife are determined to be jointly liable for an accident, their jointly held assets (including tenancy by the entirety property) will be available to satisfy such a claim. If their children acquire cars, they should be owned by and registered to the children.

Q. What types of insurance are most important for reducing risk of loss?

A. Homeowners Insurance is a must. Liability coverage up to a million dollars or more in your policy is recommended. It is relatively inexpensive. The difference between $100,000 liability protection and $1,000,000 may be under $100 per year. Automobile Insurance: Be certain the liability portion of your automobile policy is large enough. Many people remain with the same coverage for years, and are still only covered for $10,000 to $20,000 of liability. Increase your liability coverage now. Few people should have less than $100,000 coverage and those with ample assets should have $1,000,000 or more coverage per accident. Umbrella Liability: This may be the most important suggestion in this entire book for you. The majority of Americans are unaware that this type of insurance protection is available. You can add additional and broader liability coverage to your existing policies, which greatly expands the total amount of your liability coverage (usually up to $1,000,000) even though the increased premium may be exceptionally small. An umbrella policy also increases the liability coverage to other forms of liability not covered by standard home and automobile policies. For example, slander and libel are usually covered.

Q. Is it really necessary for professionals to carry malpractice policies?

A. There are two schools of thought. The conventional theory is that malpractice coverage is absolutely essential to protect family assets considering the greatly increased number of claims.

Many professionals, however, now prefer to "go bare" without insurance. These professionals believe insurance only attracts claims because plaintiffs know there are "deep pockets" to pay the claim. In fact, many doctors explicitly advise their patients that they carry no insurance in order to discourage claims. Of course, in fields such as medicine, insurance is quite expensive so costs are an important factor. Professionals who choose to "go bare" obviously have a greater need for a sound asset protection program so they remain truly judgment proof should claims occur.

Q. Is it advisable for a parent to establish a joint bank account with a child for purposes of avoiding probate?

A. Only under extreme circumstances should children be added to the title of properties owned by parents, and then only upon the advice of an attorney. Many recent case decisions allow creditors to reach assets held in joint tenancy, even though the parents' objective was to have the child's name on the property to avoid probate. For example, the United States Supreme Court stated that the Internal Revenue Service had a right to levy on a taxpayer's joint bank accounts notwithstanding that the accounts were in joint names because the taxpayer had an absolute right to compel payment of the outstanding balances in the accounts.

A fully funded trust will avoid probate just as effectively and as surely as joint tenancy, but without the dangerous side effects described.

Q. Is it advisable for two or more professionals to operate under a general partnership?

A. No. As partners each is personally liable for the negligent or wrongful acts of the other and hence the risks are too great. I strongly recommend a corporation to limit liability to the business assets.

Index